THE LITTLE BOOK OF
Trauma
Healing

Published titles include:

The Little Book of Restorative Justice, by Howard Zehr

El Pequeño Libro De Justicia Restaurativa, by Howard Zehr

The Little Book of Conflict Transformation, by John Paul Lederach

The Little Book of Family Group Conferences, New-Zealand Style,
by Allan MacRae and Howard Zehr

The Little Book of Strategic Peacebuilding, by Lisa Schirch

The Little Book of Strategic Negotiation,
by Jayne Seminare Docherty

The Little Book of Circle Processes, by Kay Pranis

The Little Book of Contemplative Photography, by Howard Zehr

The Little Book of Restorative Discipline for Schools,
by Lorraine Stutzman Amstutz and Judy H. Mullet

The Little Book of Trauma Healing, by Carolyn Yoder

The Little Book of Biblical Justice, by Chris Marshall

The Little Book of Restorative Justice for People in Prison,
by Barb Toews

The Little Book of Cool Tools for Hot Topics,
by Ron Kraybill and Evelyn Wright

The Little Book of Dialogue for Difficult Subjects,
by Lisa Schirch and David Campt

The Little Book of Victim Offender Conferencing,
by Lorraine Stutzman Amstutz

The Little Book of Healthy Organizations,
by David R. Brubaker and Ruth Hoover Zimmerman

The Little Books of Justice & Peacebuilding present, in highly accessible form, key concepts and practices from the fields of restorative justice, conflict transformation, and peacebuilding. Written by leaders in these fields, they are designed for practitioners, students, and anyone interested in justice, peace, and conflict resolution.

The Little Books of Justice & Peacebuilding series is a cooperative effort between the Center for Justice and Peacebuilding of Eastern Mennonite University (Howard Zehr, Series General Editor) and publisher Good Books (Phyllis Pellman Good, Senior Editor).

THE LITTLE BOOK OF
Trauma Healing

When Violence Strikes and
Community Security Is Threatened

CAROLYN YODER

Good　Books

Intercourse, PA 17534
800/762-7171
www.GoodBooks.com

STAR is a joint effort of Church World Service and
Eastern Mennonite University's Center for Justice and Peacebuilding.

The chart on page 33 and the diagram on page 74 are copyrighted by Eastern
Mennonite University's Center for Justice and Peacebuilding. They are used
here by permission. The sketches on pages 19 and 23 are by Lee Eshleman.

Cover photograph by Howard Zehr.
Design by Dawn J. Ranck
THE LITTLE BOOK OF TRAUMA HEALING
Copyright © 2005 by Good Books, Intercourse, PA 17534
International Standard Book Number: 978-1-56148-507-9
Library of Congress Catalog Card Number: 2005030891

Library of Congress Cataloging-in-Publication Data
Yoder, Carolyn.
The little book of trauma healing : when violence strikes and community security is threatened / Carolyn Yoder.
     p. cm.
Includes bibliographical references
ISBN 1-56148-507-1 (pbk.)
  1. Post-traumatic stress disorder--Treatment. 2. Psychic trauma--Treatment.
3. Victims--Rehabilitation. 4. Victims of crimes--Rehabilitation. 5. Victims of
terrorism--Rehabilitation. I. Title.
  RC552.P67Y63 2005
  616.85'2106--dc22   2005030891

Table of Contents

Acknowledgments

This *Little Book* is possible because many people of-
fered a piece of themselves to create a work greater
than the sum of its parts.

Janice Jenner, who directs the Center for Justice and
Peacebuilding (CJP) Practice Institute at Eastern Mennonite University, articulated the idea for the STAR
program (Strategies for Trauma Awareness and Resilience) at the request of Rick Augsburger of Church
World Service in the days after 9-11. The CJP faculty
then contributed their wisdom, experiences, theories,
and pedagogic expertise in designing and conducting
the STAR trainings. Through the highs and lows of this
process, their belief in the mission of STAR and the
common good triumphed over individualism.

Kudos to CJP faculty Jayne Docherty (human security and peacebuilding), Barry Hart (trauma healing and
peacebuilding), Vernon Jantzi (peacebuilding), Ron
Kraybill (peacebuilding), Lisa Schirch (peacebuilding),
Nancy Good Sider (trauma healing), and Howard Zehr
(restorative justice) for their ongoing contributions,
help, and support. Others who added to STAR content
include Elaine Zook Barge, Vesna Hart, Janice Jenner,
Amy Potter, Amela Puljek-Shank, and the hundreds of
STAR participants.

Through it all, I have had the privilege of serving as
the conductor of this orchestra: harmonizing the notes
of the different fields, bringing the score of my own experience in trauma healing and neurobiology, keeping

attuned to audience response, and marveling at the swells of the music and how it travels.

Thanks to STAR staff Sharon Forret, Kathy Smith, and Robert Yutzy for their support services; to Jennifer Larson Sawin, Janet Loker, and Ira Weiss for reading and critiquing the manuscript; to Howard Zehr and Jayne Docherty for critiquing and assisting in the justice and peacebuilding sections; and to Lam Cosmas, Marie Mitchell, and Jean Handley for the gift of their personal stories.

Thanks also to Howard Zehr and Good Books for their encouragement and editorial work, and to Church World Service for the multiple levels of support that helped to initiate and implement STAR. Special thanks to my husband Rick, whose support included taking over the care of the goats and many other things around home while I was writing.

1.
Introduction

How can we effectively address the threat of terrorism?
What helps bring about long-term security?
What stops cycles of victimhood and violence?
And what does trauma have to do with all of this?

The last century may have been the most brutal in human history, measured by the number of people affected by violence. Early in the new millennium, hundreds of conflicts continue to rage across the planet. Yet as our fractured global family struggles to find answers, little is said about the links between trauma, security, and violence.

Trauma and violence are integrally linked.

Politicians, negotiators, peacebuilders, and the general public alike tend to think of trauma healing as soft, a warm fuzzy that has little or nothing to do with realpolitik and no role to play in reducing violence. Yet trauma and violence are integrally linked: violence often leads to trauma, and unhealed trauma, in turn, can lead to violence and further loss of security.

Trauma affects our very physiology, including our ability to do integrated, whole-brain thinking. John Gottman's research on couples and predictors of marital success or failure has found that when our pulse raises as few as 10 beats above our usual baseline, the rational part of our brain begins slipping out of gear.[1] We then begin talking, acting, and reacting from the lower part of our brain where our automatic survival instincts are located.

If this physiological change occurs over disagreements about who cleans up the kitchen, what happens when political debates rage, terrorists attack, or negotiators discuss disputed territory at a bargaining table? Understanding trauma—physiologically, emotionally, mentally, and spiritually—may help to explain a wide range of phenomenon, including feelings of insecurity, loss of cultural identity, racism or extreme nationalism, and violence in general.

Trauma as a call to change and transformation

But there is another side to trauma. Indeed, the primary premise and challenge of this *Little Book* is that traumatic events and times have the potential to awaken the best of the human spirit and, indeed, the global family. This is not an automatic process, however. It requires that we acknowledge our own history *and our enemy's,* search honestly for root causes, and shift our emphasis from national security to human security. At the core, it is spiritual work of the deepest sort, calling forth nothing less than the noblest ideals and the faith, hope, and resilience of the human spirit.

About this book

In the aftermath of events on September 11, 2001, The Center for Justice and Peacebuilding (CJP) at Eastern Mennonite University, and Church World Service, the relief and development agency of 38 religious groups, worked together to better equip religious and civil-society leaders for dealing with traumatic situations. One of the outcomes is a program called STAR—Strategies for

Trauma Awareness and Resilience—that brings together middle and grassroots leaders from areas of conflict in the United States and around the world for seminars that are both experiential and academic.

STAR integrates concepts from traditionally separate fields of study and practice: traumatology (including neurobiology), human security, restorative justice, conflict transformation, peacebuilding, and faith/spirituality. Tying it all together is a three-part model called The Trauma Healing Journey: Breaking the Cycles of Victimhood and Violence.

We adapted this model from the work of the Center for Strategic International Studies in Washington, D.C., which with David Steele, Olga Botcharova, Barry Hart, and others conducted workshops in the former Yugoslavia in the late 1990s. We are indebted to them for their pioneering work.[2]

Change begins with me, with you, with us.

Obviously this approach goes beyond the traditional mental health medical model, which focuses on individual trauma. Instead, the primary emphasis is on communities and societies caught up in cycles of victimhood and/or violence, although many of the concepts are readily adaptable and applicable to individuals. Indeed, the STAR approach is based on helping people understand and heal from traumatic events, while helping to develop societal and structural responses that address the causes and consequences of conflict and violence. It explores how to think about and respond to traumatic events—including terrorism—so that communities do not get caught in a cycle of tit-for-tat violence or see themselves as perpetual victims.

Although the concepts explored here apply to a whole spectrum of traumatic events, STAR initially arose as a response to an act of terrorism. Later the model was adapted further to apply to natural disasters such as the tsunami of 2004 and Hurricane Katrina in 2005.

The term "terrorism" is often used loosely, but according to Cunningham,[3] it has four key elements:

1. It involves an act in which violence or force is used or threatened.

2. It is primarily a political act.

3. It is intended to cause fear or terror.

4. The goal is to achieve psychological effects and reactions.

Objectivity breaks down when talking about terrorism precisely because terrorist acts engender an emotionally charged trauma response in the victims, in their communities, and in those who sympathize with them.

This is not a book of answers but of information, ideas, theories, and questions emerging from our experiences. The question of how to work toward human security in these turbulent times without adding to the violence and trauma of our world is a huge topic without definitive answers. Sometimes it seems naive to address the question of security in the face of enormous problems. But change begins with me, with you, with us, as together we explore, observe, listen, imagine, pray, experiment, and learn.

2.
Defining Trauma:
The Causes and Types

The tranquility of Lam Cosmas' growing-up years in Northern Uganda was shattered in 1986 when rebels began raiding cattle and attacking unarmed civilians. Over the next years villages were sacked, crops burned, and men and women killed. Nighttime raids took boys as young as seven to be child soldiers and the girls to be "wives" to the rebels. Terrified, the villagers moved to the urban centers in droves where they continue to live crowded in camps for internally displaced persons, lacking in basic amenities.

* * *

On September 11, 2001, Marie Mitchell was at work in her California office when a neighbor called and told her to turn on the TV. As she watched the World Trade Towers go up in flames and then collapse, Marie slumped from her chair to the floor. Her brother was a firefighter in southern Manhattan. She knew he would be there.

* * *

Jinnah works long days to support his family as a rickshaw driver in the crowded streets of Dhaka, Bangladesh. He pedals his passengers in the heat of the dry season and through the warm monsoon rains that flood the streets. He works when he feels well and when has a fever, when he

---

*has eaten or when he is hungry. Two of his six children
have died of diarrhea-related causes. He has given up
hope of sending the surviving children to school: he cannot
afford the fees for books and uniforms. Jinnah has stopped
thinking about tomorrow.*

* * *

*A.L.M. Thaseem lost his wife and his two children in
the 2004 tsunami in Southeast Asia,which also destroyed
his business and heavily damaged his house. New rules by
the Sri Lankan government to discourage people from living near the sea mean he cannot rebuild his guest house
business or repair his home, leaving him in limbo.[4]*

The four vignettes above are quite different.[5] But all
result in some degree of trauma reaction for the individuals and the societies in which they occur.

In casual conversation, the word trauma is used to describe reactions to anything from a stressful day to a brutal murder. Indeed, both stress and trauma do affect individuals and groups physically, emotionally, cognitively,
behaviorally, and spiritually. But traumatic events differ
from ordinary stress in intensity and/or duration.

Traumatic events:

- Involve threats to lives or bodies.
- Produce terror and feelings of helplessness.
- Overwhelm an individual's or group's ability to
  cope or respond to the threat.
- Lead to a sense of loss of control.
- Challenge a person's or group's sense that life is
  meaningful and orderly.

Whether or not a situation is overwhelming cannot be determined by looking only at the events. What is merely stressful for one individual or group of people may be traumatic for another, depending on a combination of factors. These include age, previous history, degree of preparation, the meaning given to the event, how long it lasts, the quality of social support available, knowledge about how to deal with trauma, genetic makeup, and spiritual centeredness. *Consequently, a traumatic reaction needs to be treated as valid, regardless of how the event that induced it appears to anyone else.*

Traumas occur in a context, a social setting, with dynamic interactions between the individual and the surrounding society.[6] The social conditions and meanings of an individual experience often cause or contribute to trauma.

For example, Kadzu has AIDS which she contracted from her husband, who had died a year earlier. She and her two sons live with her elderly widowed mother and are financially dependent on their extended family. Kadzu's situation is impacted by the attitude of her family, community, and nation toward AIDS; by the resources available for prevention and treatment; and by the intellectual property rights, drug prices, and patents of multinational pharmaceutical companies. The latter, in turn, are affected by international trade agreements. Similarly, Lam's and Jinnah's trauma is induced by the social environment in which they live.

Ongoing and structurally-induced trauma

Not all trauma is induced by single dramatic events that are outside the normal range of human experience, such as a tornado or an accident or even the death of Marie's brother in the World Trade Center. Trauma can be caused by living under abusive or unsafe conditions that are long-term and continuous. This is the case with the ongoing civil war in Lam's story or the struggle to survive in Jinnah's. Conditions that at one time were rare, such as muggings, rape, and gang activities, are now ordinary in many parts of the world. The constant possibility of death or injury in conflict zones, or where populations live under occupation and in fear of terrorism, are no less traumatic because they are routine. The ongoing violence of poverty and systems that make people unable to meet basic needs such as healthcare is called *structural violence* and is a cause of trauma. Often these structural-induced traumas go unnoticed until an event such as Hurricane Katrina graphically exposes what has existed all along.

> Trauma may be induced by ongoing, routine events or conditions.

There is no standard term in trauma literature for this experience of living with ongoing trauma. It has been called *cumulative trauma; continuous trauma; chronic trauma; sequential, multiple,* or *plural traumas.* Perhaps Martha Cabrera, who works on trauma recovery programs in Nicaragua, describes it best when she refers to her society as multiply wounded, multiply traumatized, and multiply grieving after experiencing several decades of conflict.[7] The psychological, spiritual, social, economic, and political effects of these ongoing difficult conditions can be profound, not only for individuals but for entire societies.[8]

Societal or collective trauma

When a traumatic event or series of events affects large numbers of people, we speak of *societal* or *collective trauma.* Trauma may be directly experienced, but it can also occur when witnessing (e.g. on television) or merely hearing about horrific events. Whether direct or indirect, a group experience of trauma can set off widespread fear, horror, helplessness, or anger. Such events are not merely private experiences but have impact at national and regional levels, resulting in societal trauma.

Some of these are specific to the culture or society. For example, "September 11" instantly evokes images of the attacks on New York City and Washington, D.C., in 2001 for U.S. citizens as well as many others. In Chile, however, "September 11" evokes the trauma of the September 11, 1973 U.S.-backed overthrow of the democratically-elected government of Salvador Allende. Many in Central America remember the September 11, 1990 stabbing of Guatemalan anthropologist Myrna Mack who was documenting human rights abuses.

> Unaddressed traumas affect not only those directly traumatized, but their families and future generations.

Within a single society, cultural subgroups may experience events differently, depending on their proximity to the threat or their identity with the victims of the events.

Historical trauma transferred through generations

Historical trauma is the "cumulative emotional and psychological wounding over the lifespan and across generations emanating from massive group trauma."[9] Slavery, colonialism, and persecution or genocide of one faction or religious group are examples. The "event" or institution is in the past, but the effects are cumulative and are seen in individual and group attitudes and behaviors in succeeding generations. The trans-generational transmission of these traumas can occur even when the next generation is not told the trauma story, or knows it only in broad outline. A "conspiracy of silence" surrounds events for which grieving and mourning have never taken place.

Cultural traumas are created when attempts are made to eradicate part or all of a culture or people. This has happened for many native and indigenous groups worldwide.

Secondary trauma

Secondary or *vicarious trauma* refers to the effects experienced by rescue workers, caregivers, and others who respond to catastrophes and attend to direct victims firsthand. Many journalists who covered victims' testimonies in South Africa's Truth and Reconciliation Commission reported post-traumatic stress reactions, even though they were briefed beforehand on how to avoid becoming personally traumatized. The effects of secondary trauma are similar to those experienced by victims and survivors themselves.

Participation-induced trauma

Another cause of trauma is rarely discussed: being an active participant in causing harm or trauma to others, whether in the line of duty or outside of the law, such as in criminal activity. Psychologist Rachael MacNair's research suggests that the traumatic effects of harming others, intentionally or unintentionally, can be as severe as or more severe than what victims and survivors experience.[10]

The issues MacNair raises likely have significance for communities, groups, and nations. What are the emotional and spiritual implications for groups or nations that bear responsibility for events such as the holocaust, genocide, suicide bombings, state-supported assassinations, or preemptive wars?

In summary

Traumatic events and situations overwhelm our usual ability to cope with and respond to threat. The following are common traumatic events or stressors:

- Abuse or assault: physical, emotional, sexual (including rape)
- Accidents
- Causing harm to others deliberately: criminals; torturers; abusers; terrorists including state-sponsored or -sanctioned terrorism; abuse of power
- Causing harm to others in the line of duty: law enforcement, executioners, military personnel
- Economic policies, poverty
- Homelessness, being a refugee
- Human-caused disasters: chemical spills, dams or levees that break
- Living under occupation or in conditions of servitude or slavery
- Mass violence: assaults, massacres, genocide, wars
- Natural disasters: hurricanes, earthquakes, tornados, tsunamis
- Neglect of those who cannot care for themselves
- Serious illnesses, pandemics and epidemics such as AIDS, bioterrorism
- Structural violence: social structures and institutions that deprive people of their rights and ability to meet basic needs
- Sudden loss of loved ones, status, identity, possessions, home, territory

- Sudden changing of the rules, expectations, or norms; social revolutions
- Surgical, dental, and medical procedures, including difficult births
- Torture
- Witnessing death or injury

In short, there are many causes and types of trauma. We turn now to the ways we as individuals and societies respond to traumatic events.

3.
Common Responses to Traumatic Events

L am Cosmas remembers the date clearly: October 3, 1986. *I lived in Gulu, and I boarded a bus that morning to travel to the capital, Kampala. I was sitting near the center of the bus, and I got uneasy when we came to a spot about 16 kilometers from town because rebels had attacked a truck there not long ago. Then through the window I saw people in military fatigues squatting beside the road with their guns pointed. I was so afraid. I screamed at the driver, "Don't stop, don't stop." I heard bullets and the screams of the other passengers. I couldn't keep from shouting, "Don't stop!"*

The driver roared the engine and sped down the road. I just remember some things: blood everywhere, people screaming, the face of a man hit in the jaw, a man whose legs were shot up. I was so scared I didn't know if I was hurt or not. And the children. Some of them were under the seats. It was odd. They did not cry out or make a sound.

The driver stopped when we got to the next town, about 50 kilometers from the scene. I checked my body—no injuries. Those hurt were taken to a hospital. No one died, but the man with the leg wounds had both legs amputated. We inspected the bus and found bullet holes right above the tires. Thank God they didn't hit the tires. Then we noticed that the driver's trousers were bloody: he had been shot. You know, he hadn't felt any pain.

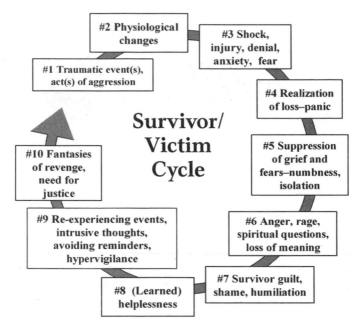

Based on a model by Olga Botcharova © 1988, from *Forgiveness and Reconciliation,* Templeton Foundation Press. Used by permission. This adaptation of Botcharova's model © by Eastern Mennonite University, Center for Justice and Peacebuilding, 2002. Used by permission.

To track and understand the way trauma, violence, and security are interrelated, we will use three interlinking diagrams throughout the book that together make up the model we call The Trauma Healing Journey: Breaking the Cycles of Victimhood and Violence. The first of these, the Survivor/Victim Cycle, depicts common, normal trauma responses when violence shatters our sense of security. The numbers in parentheses throughout the text refer to the numbers on the diagram. *Note that although the reactions in this cycle are numbered sequentially, in real life they do not necessarily happen one at a time or in a neat linear order.*

Trauma affects us physiologically

The brain plays a key role in how we respond to trauma (see #1-2). The three major interdependent parts of the brain are:

- The *cerebral cortex:* our rational, thinking brain.
- The *limbic system:* the "emotional brain," memory storage, and emotion; contains the *amygdala,* a "first-alert system" that is activated by fear.
- The *brain stem:* our "instinctual brain" which

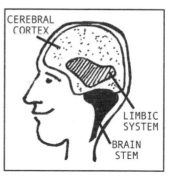

controls automatic reactions, including the fight, flight, or freeze response. It has no sense of linear time; everything is "now" to this part of the brain.

The limbic system and brain stem are sometimes referred to as the *lower brain,* and the cerebral cortex is called the *higher brain.*

Under normal conditions, incoming information is routed first to the cerebral cortex, our rational brain, and then on to the lower brain. But in a crisis, as when Lam sees the guns pointed at the bus, the information bypasses the thinking centers of the brain and goes directly to the amygdala, which registers FEAR.

This first-alert alarm in the brain's limbic system instantaneously triggers the release of a cascade of stress chemicals and hormones. This activates the fight-or-flight response in the brain stem and puts the body in a state of hyperarousal in order to save our lives.[11] Heart rate, respiration, and metabolism increase. Blood rushes to the muscles and other parts of the body to produce extra strength and energy. Functions not needed for survival, such as digestion, shut down. Those needed to stay alive, such as sight, are sharpened.

Dissociation, a distancing from what is happening, protects us from being overwhelmed by the full emotional impact or by the physical pain in the moment. Time is distorted: things happen in slow motion or in an accelerated rush. Some people experience a sense of quiet, detached calm.

Memories are not processed or stored in the usual way. They become fragmented, later producing graphic images on the one hand, and, paradoxically, an inability to recall on the other. The parts of the brain controlling speech shut down, giving rise to expressions such as "mute with terror."

The arousal in response to threat is produced for running away or fighting to survive. This completes a natural physiological cycle. If the cycle completes, we feel a sense of relief, even triumph and exhilaration: the body calms down and returns to a state of rest. However, when running away or fighting is impossible (as when Lam was trapped on the bus), or when the combination of terror and helplessness is overwhelming, the body may go into a freeze response. We are unable to think, move, or even talk. Freezing when the tornado-like energy of fight-or-flight still has the nervous system in a state of hyperarousal is like pressing on the accelerator of a car while slamming on the brakes.

Freezing traps the intense trauma energy in the nervous system.

Freezing traps the intense trauma energy in the nervous system. If it is not discharged or integrated within a few days or weeks, this constriction of energy is believed to be what produces common trauma reactions later, not the actual event itself.[12]

Lam continues:

Those of us who were not hurt continued on the three hours to Kampala. I don't remember much about the trip, except that near the end, one of the tires burst with a loud

POP that sounded like a gunshot. Everyone screamed and crouched down in the seats. It was awful.

Later, when I told my family what happened, I was trembling and perspiring. I had dreams about it for near-ly three months, and I thought about it a lot, even though I tried not to. All these years later, I still feel fear when I pass the spot where it happened.

Brain researchers tell us that neurons that fire togeth-er wire together. Neurons are specialized cells of the ner-vous system that carry "messages" through an electro-chemical process. The more intense the experience is, the tighter they wire together.

Later, sounds, sights, smells, or even dynamics that we experience which are similar to the original trauma can cause time to collapse and the trauma memory to come back vividly and unbidden. These are called intrusive memories (#9). We respond as if the event were happening now.

Consequently, survivors seek to avoid these triggers, or reminders of what happened, so that they do not ex-perience frighteningly vivid intrusive memories or flash-backs. This can cause them to withdraw from life.

For the passengers on Lam's bus, the emotion of fear wired with the sound of gunshots, the smell and sight of blood, the moans of the injured. The sound of the tire blow-ing instantly triggered memories of the original attack.

The shaking and sweating Lam experienced are natural physical trauma responses. They result from the tornado-like energy that is frozen inside and continues to be gener-ated by thoughts and memories of what happened. When survivors can be helped to discharge this energy, many post-traumatic reactions such as nightmares and flash-backs are minimized or resolved.[13] But our higher, rational brain often gets in the way of listening to our bodies. We're afraid the shaking and overwhelming feelings mean we're going crazy or falling apart, and so we "hold ourselves together," thus suppressing these natural, healing responses along with our grief and fears (#5).

The intense trauma energy of hyper-arousal can also show up as anger or rage directed at whatever or whoever is closest: the rescue squad that didn't respond fast enough, the doctor who should have tried harder, the disaster agency that should have provided more assistance, the spouse who isn't empathic enough, the ethnic group of the attackers (#6). The anger may or may not be justified, but the intensity is frequently out of proportion.

Marie describes an incident that happened soon after her brother's memorial service which took place about two months after his death.

> *I was feeling shaky, so I drove to a park to take a walk. A man was there with two dogs and I asked him to put them on a leash. He told me I needed to be on a leash. I got so angry I wanted to run the man down with my car, to just roar at him with the engine. I actually started driving toward him. I could really have run the guy down. I don't know what was in me, but I wanted the engine to ROAR for me. I wanted to plow through the whole known universe and this man was the center, the bull's eye. But even the universe wasn't enough. I wanted to roar on out into space, into the galaxy and nebulae and on into the void.*

In everyday language, we would say Marie "lost it." Physiologically, that's accurate. The "it" Marie lost is the "connection" to her rational brain.

To live as emotionally intelligent human beings, we need all parts of our brain to work together. The orbitofrontal cortex, located in the region behind our eyes, links and integrates the three major regions of the brain: the cerebral cortex (rational brain), limbic system (emotional brain), and brain stem (instinctual brain).[14] Among other things, it allows us to regulate emotions, read nonverbal communication cues, take in information from around us, reflect on that information before acting, be flexible, have empathy for others, and act ethically and with kindness.[15]

But neuroscientists believe trauma disrupts the orbitofrontal cortex functioning, leaving us susceptible to what interpersonal neurobiology expert Daniel Siegel calls "low-mode" (lower brain) states. Rational thought is hijacked. Without this integration, we experience intense emotions, impulsive reactions, and rigid and repetitive responses. Our ability to be self reflective and to consider another person's or group's point of view is impaired.[16]

In Marie's story, her orbitofrontal cortex has engaged when she recalls:

> Then a little voice said, "Marie, turn the car around. Go home." I was really shaking, but I turned the car around and drove home. I thought, "I need to meditate."

The rage process reverses and she can choose either to run the man down or turn around. She chose to listen to the still small voice and turn around.

Given the intensity of trauma responses, it's easy to understand why we feel overwhelmed and out of control. It's easy to understand why we suppress feelings (#5) and retreat into emotional numbness and denial of what happened

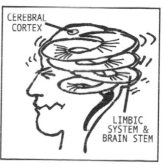

or its effects on us. At first this can seem like a healthy defense, as it keeps us from being overwhelmed. If it continues, however, it negatively affects relationships and our ability to live life to the fullest.

Trauma shatters meaning

Traumatic events shatter the world as we know it, leaving us disordered, disempowered, and feeling disconnected from other people and from life. Our response may be anger, anxiety, depression, and asking questions that are both personal and global: Why us? Where was God? And, what is the meaning of life anyway? (#6).

Marie describes her experience:

> *The anger was so nondescript. It was not about the terrorists but about the whole system, about where we as a human race have gone. And I was angry at myself. Because in spite of all the prayer and meditation I've done, I was reacting like this. At some irrational level I thought, "How can my life up to now have any value, any good, if these feelings are so powerful?" My feelings came in waves, but for a long time, I felt like I was on the verge of a nervous breakdown.*

The depth of feeling, thoughts, and reactions can be frightening, even overwhelming. The losses—of loved ones, homes, jobs, community, status, and security—lead us to question our core identity. When we feel out of control or "unspiritual," we tend to suppress the grief, pain, and questions (#4, 5, 7, 8). Feelings of shame, self-blame, and humiliation are common. So is guilt at surviving when others have died (#7).

Although it is not logical, we may believe we should have been able to prevent or overcome whatever happened, or that if we were somehow better people we wouldn't feel so bad now. In part, what is at stake is a sense of honor. We feel shame that it happened to us. And if we don't understand normal trauma responses, we are ashamed about how we have responded. As the reality of our losses break through the initial shock and denial, we can feel as if we are on the verge of going crazy.

We are meaning-making creatures, and we find much *storytelling* of our identity and security in the meaning we give to the world. These meanings are often embedded in our life stories. When trauma shatters our world, our meaning, our stories, are disrupted: Indeed, this attack on our as- sumptions—or our meaning and stories—is part of what causes trauma. Thus, we look for ways to explain what happened, and we tell our stories as a way to recreate our sense of meaning and identity.

Trauma creates needs

As this suggests, people who have been traumatized need to know and understand what happened. They of- ten desire information, but they also may need opportu- nities to tell their stories. Trauma often creates a need to "restory" our lives.

However, the most urgent need for trauma survivors is often for safety and security—physically, emotionally, and spiritually. We want to know that steps are being taken to prevent the recurrence of what happened. We also want answers, not only because they give meaning but because they offer a sense of order and therefore security. If we know who did something and why, for example, it may make life seem a bit more predictable. As we shall see, when we don't have good answers, we often resort to sim- ple and inaccurate answers to give meaning and security.

Traumatic situations often leave us feeling that we have been victimized and treated unjustly (#10). Work with crime victims has identified some of the "justice needs" on the part of those who have experienced this sense of injustice.[17]

Justice needs of victims
- safety
- information, answers
- story-telling/truth-telling
- empowerment
- vindication
- restitution

An important need by those who feel victimized is vindication. All of us seem to have a basic need for reciprocity, to balance the score; this is as true for giving and receiving gifts as it for righting wrongs.

Part of this is a moral balancing: we want to know that we are not to blame and that someone else is accepting responsibility. Part of it involves removing the shame and humiliation that accompanies victimization and, ideally, replacing it with a sense of honor and respect. Sometimes this can be addressed, at least in part, by apologies and restitution. Even if the actual losses are impossible to compensate, there may be a need for some symbolic statement or reparation.

Another need is for empowerment: trauma takes away our sense of power and control, leaving in its wake humiliation and shame. This needs to be replaced with a sense of dignity and personal power or autonomy.

Experiences of justice, whether direct or symbolic, often play a critical part in the healing journey of those who have been traumatized. Vicious revenge fantasies are common when these justice needs are not met.

As noted in the last chapter, traumatic events such as Hurricane Katrina can expose and magnify pre-existing structural violence and injustice. The justice needs arising out of traumatic events then compound those that existed before.

Ongoing trauma

In environments of continuous trauma, characteristics that are considered unhealthy in the months after a single traumatic event can be signs of adaptive coping needed to survive ongoing or multiple traumas.[18] For example, hypervigilance keeps people alive in a crime-ridden neighborhood, when living under military occupation, or while on patrol in a war zone. Emotional numbing and denial helps to keep the hopelessness of a situation at bay, enabling adults to go to work and children to go to school under harrowing circumstances.

> Trauma can either strengthen or undermine community.

Such adaptations may be "normal" but does not mean that they are healthy over time. Long-term stress reactions include changes in the way we think about ourselves, the way we perceive those who hurt us, our relations with others, our ability to regulate our emotions, and our system of meaning.

Judith Lewis Herman says that those who experience single traumas often feel they may be losing their minds, but those who undergo long-term trauma often feel they have lost themselves.[19] This has serious implications for people's health, the resilience of a society's social fabric, the success of development schemes, and the hope of future generations.[20]

In some situations of ongoing trauma, a strong sense of community develops as people band together to help each other. As the next section outlines, the opposite can also happen: trust between people can break down under the duress of economic, political, and social instability. People can become suspicious of or hostile toward others, especially those who are different. Politicians sometimes deliberately create situations that destroy trust. As insecurity rises and identities are threatened, people may retreat into their own clans or tight-knit communities of religion, ethnicity, or kin.

Large-group trauma

Large-group traumas that directly impact entire groups or societies include natural disasters, human-caused accidents, and acts of deliberate harm—or a combination of these. (Hurricane Katrina and the 2004 tsunami are examples of this.) Vamik Volkan has spent several decades working with socio-political conflicts of large groups and studying the effects of large-group trauma on present and future societies in various parts of the world.

The most difficult traumas are those deliberately caused.

Volkan describes the common reactions to natural disasters as shock, chaos, survivor guilt, and preoccupation with images of death and destruction, which often last for months or even years. Survivors experience a lingering, shared anxiety from having lost trust in "Mother Nature." After a time of mourning, regeneration takes place.[21] Clearly, the magnitude and nature of the disaster affects how long this process takes. The sheer scope of tragedies such as the 2004 tsunami or Hurricane Katrina will have long-lasting effects.

In disasters caused by human failures—the radioactive leakage at Chernobyl, or the collapse of a poorly constructed apartment building, or the collapse of the sea wall in New Orleans—blame is often placed on a small number of individuals, a corporation, or governmental organizations. Although others bear some culpability—and greed or neglect may have been involved—it makes a difference to us that no one *deliberately* sought to cause harm. Damage settlements help those impacted to feel a sense of vindication.[22]

> The past
> is not dead.
> In fact,
> it's not
> even past.
>
> – William Faulkner

According to Volkan, the most difficult traumas are those deliberately caused by others.[23] The cruelty of calculated harm impacts us intensely. Frequently this leads to a predictable series of counter-moves from the victims that can start cycles of violence. We respond with fear, rage, helplessness, humiliation, increased group identity, and a desire for vindication. We have a need for justice, and when our justice needs are ignored, we may seek revenge. Without an experience of justice, deliberate acts of harm often become "chosen traumas," a shared traumatic event that is "chosen" to be kept alive through the generations and becomes an integral part of a group's identity. Chosen traumas are characterized by an obsessive sense of being wronged by the "other" and by a sense of entitlement.[24]

These after-effects of trauma bring us to the next chapter: the cycle of unhealed trauma.

4.
Continuing the Cycles: Unhealed Trauma

"Pain that is not transformed is transferred."
—Richard Rohr

When the violence of trauma—whether from terrorism or tsunamis—shatters our security, we stand at a crossroad. We can begin to transform the suffering into something meaningful and restorative, a gift to the world. This is the focus of Chapter 5.

> When traumatic events happen, we stand at a crossroad.

In the present chapter, however, we will examine the other road too frequently traveled, where normal trauma reactions morph into destructive cycles of victimhood or violence. The results of this choice are evident daily in the media and in the stories individuals or groups tell of an illness or a death, loss, betrayal, battle, or war. The themes are suffering, injustice, fear, hopelessness, powerlessness, shame, humiliation, rage, retaliation, and hatred.

Fred Luskin calls these repetitive narratives "grievance stories."[25] Individuals and groups with unchanging grievance stories are stuck. The normal, common reactions to trauma, discussed in the last chapter, endure, morphing into destructive cycles of victimhood or violence.

Using the Enemy/Aggressor Cycle on page 38, we will examine these cycles of unhealed individual and large-group traumas, including some of the complex contributing factors. We will see how this can lead those who have suffered to begin deadly cycles of tit-for-tat violence with consequences for months, years, and even centuries. But first, a word about the commonly used framework for understanding unhealed trauma: post-traumatic stress disorder (PTSD).

Limitations of defining unhealed trauma through a PTSD frame

Post-traumatic stress disorder (PTSD) is a diagnosis given to individuals by medical and mental-health professionals when severe reactions or symptoms of trauma last longer than one month. The symptoms include persistent re-experiencing of the traumatic event, persistent avoidance of stimuli associated with the event, numbing of general responsiveness, and persistent symptoms of increased arousal.[26]

There is ongoing discussion about how useful this diagnosis is and how widely it should be used, especially in large-scale events, ongoing traumas, and with non-Western societies. It is generally accepted that a small percentage of a population will have severe reactions and need mental health care. But broad use of the diagnosis is seen by some as pathologizing normal responses to traumatic situations.

However, there is also a danger that trauma responses in populations may be *underestimated* and therefore minimized if PTSD is the standard by which trauma is measured. As we saw earlier, trauma impacts body, mind, and spirit. In the midst of ongoing trauma or in the wake of a traumatic event, individuals and groups may appear calm and "normal" with only mild post-traumatic reactions, or none at all.

Human beings are enormously resilient and many will genuinely cope well. However, if the trauma is not addressed, or is ongoing, many people may experience a frozen numbness (constriction) or internal hyperarousal, or alternate between the two. The "proof" is not the absence of post-traumatic reactions, nor in the ability to carry out basic functions (e.g. to continue going to school or work). It is in the *quality* of relationships and in the behavior of individuals, communities, and societies in the months, years, and centuries that follow. We need to look at the how the trauma shows itself in reenactment behaviors in individuals, groups, and societies to understand the full impact of traumatic events or times.

Reenactment and trigger events

Reenactment behaviors—those that turn unhealed trauma energy against the self (acting-in) or out on others (acting out)—are signs of distress and unhealed trauma[27] (see page 33). These signs of trouble often (unconsciously) intensify around the anniversary of the traumatic event. Paradoxically, reenactments represent attempts to resolve the effects of trauma. Reenactment behaviors are a major public health issue and indicate that people and groups need psychosocial and spiritual help.

The effects of unhealed trauma can often be seen in the way a seemingly minor event—a smell, gesture, tone of voice, group dynamic, or symbol—can trigger an intrusive reaction or a conscious or unconscious memory that propels us into a low-mode brain reaction. The longer trauma is unaddressed, the greater the likelihood that the "fire-to-

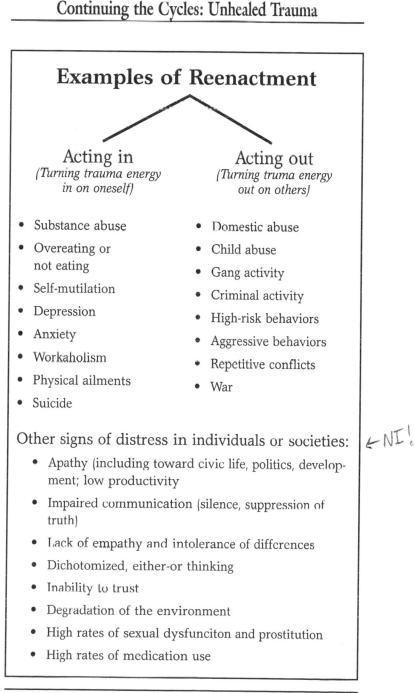

Examples of Reenactment

Acting in
*(Turning trauma energy
in on oneself)*

- Substance abuse
- Overeating or
  not eating
- Self-mutilation
- Depression
- Anxiety
- Workaholism
- Physical ailments
- Suicide

Acting out
*(Turning truma energy
out on others)*

- Domestic abuse
- Child abuse
- Gang activity
- Criminal activity
- High-risk behaviors
- Aggressive behaviors
- Repetitive conflicts
- War

Other signs of distress in individuals or societies: ← NI!

- Apathy (including toward civic life, politics, development; low productivity
- Impaired communication (silence, suppression of truth)
- Lack of empathy and intolerance of differences
- Dichotomized, either-or thinking
- Inability to trust
- Degradation of the environment
- High rates of sexual dysfunciton and prostitution
- High rates of medication use

gether-wire-together" neural pathways will strengthen, becoming our default means of responding. As we continue in a state of hypervigilance from unhealed trauma, our rational brains can become irrational and give "threat" meaning even to benign actions of other people or groups.

Impaired functioning

As we have seen, trauma disrupts the ability of the orbitofrontal cortex to help us function as thoughtful, emotionally intelligent individuals. Neurobiology research has focused primarily on individuals rather than groups or societies. However, both Martha Cabrera's and Vamik Volkan's descriptions of societies dealing with large-scale or ongoing traumas are strikingly parallel to the descriptions of individuals with impaired function.

In chapter 3, we saw that these included regulating emotions, including fear responses of the limbic brain; being flexible; feeling empathy for the pain of others; being self-aware; and acting ethically and with altruism. In Carbrera's Nicaragua, after decades of conflict, she sees a reduced ability to communicate, reduced ability to be flexible and tolerant, and loss of trust between people. She also sees apathy, isolation, aggressiveness, chronic somatic illness, increases in domestic violence and suicide, and an inability to see history through the eyes of another.[28]

Volkan has observed that societies with extensive trauma and conflict typically exhibit what John Mack has called the "egoism of victimization";[29] that is, the inability to see beyond one's own pain to empathize with the suffering of others. Consequently, there is little guilt about committing retaliatory violence and a failure to take responsibility for the victims and suffering created by one's own actions.[30]

Incomplete grieving

Healthy mourning and grieving is key to trauma heal-ing, whether from individual losses, the effects of terror-ism, or natural disasters. Mourning allows us to break through the immobility, numbness, or suppression that at first defended us from unbearable pain.

Grieving and mourning unfreezes our body, mind, and spirit so that we can think creatively, feel fully, and move forward again. However, grief frequently gets thwarted for a number of reasons.

Healthy mourning and grieving are key to trauma healing.

First, the intensity of the feelings as we let go of the numbness and denial can feel overwhelming, even like death. The feel-ings range from humiliation to rage, fear, and despair. So the trauma continues to be suppressed as we try to be strong, "get over it," and move on. However, anger of-ten smolders just beneath the surface. Brain studies show that anger and rage block the ability to feel grief, further complicating the mourning process.

Second, we cannot mourn what we will not acknowl-edge. Perhaps "our side" has lost or lost face. Perhaps we have "won" but we fear that grieving our losses somehow means "the other" has gotten something over on us. Sometimes knowing the truth about what happened can seem to destroy the last shred of hope.[31]

Third, acknowledgment is an exercise in truth-telling and as such can threaten the social, economic, or politi-cal order. For example, families frequently minimize a substance-abuse problem or turn against the member who exposes abuse for fear it will upset their world. At a national level, those who seek to bring atrocities or less-than-honorable events or policies to light can be labeled unpatriotic. Worse, they may be discredited, silenced, or even killed.

Fourth, in some circumstances it is not possible to know what happened, as with unsolved crimes, soldiers who are captured or missing in action, suicides, or detainees held incognito. Such situations create what Pauline Boss calls "ambiguous grief" or "frozen sadness" for loved ones and the wider society.[32] Even if survivors want to know the truth, acknowledgment can only happen in stages and phases, as information becomes available.

Fifth, mourning and grieving can also be thwarted if the traumatic events are ongoing and acute, as in parts of the Middle East or West Africa. The focus is on survival, as concerns for day-to-day security supercede all else.

Sixth, grieving can also be affected by not having the body of a deceased loved one, or by seeing a family member buried in a mass grave, as after the 2004 tsunami, without the usual cultural and religious rituals.

Marie shares from her story:

> *As soon as they allowed planes to fly again, I went back to New York. We went through what to do when there are no remains. I put it in the frame that my brother was basically cremated, and I don't have a problem with cremation. But even so, it affected me. No body, no gravesite. It must be one of the most difficult things people face worldwide, when someone dies far from home or when there's a mass burial, or no remains.*

Regardless of the reasons for incomplete mourning, the resulting frozen grief thwarts healing and keeps populations more susceptible to acting out of low-mode

---

Obstacles to Mourning

- Fear of being overwhelmed
- Inability to face what happened
- Threats to the known "order"
- Truth that is unknowable
- Trauma that is ongoing
- Inability to carry out usual rituals

---

brain states. Normal fear can morph into panic and paranoia, pain into despair, anger into rage, humiliation and shame into an obsessive drive for vindication. The quest for measured justice can be confused with retaliation and revenge. These patterns and frustrations are intensified if the justice needs, summarized in Chapter 3, are not met. Even more frightening, we are more susceptible to meaning-making narratives that can lead us from being victim/survivors to aggressors.

The enemy/aggressor cycle[33]

When trauma shatters our world, we look for ways to explain what happened. We tell stories or narratives that attempt to give meaning to the events. Under the duress of threat, fear, grief, and unmet needs, we often unconsciously latch onto familiar narratives and follow them unreflectively. The following are two narrative patterns that we commonly fall back on in these situations:

Common narratives:
- good vs. evil
- redemptive violence

Enemy/Aggressor & Survivor/Victim Cycles

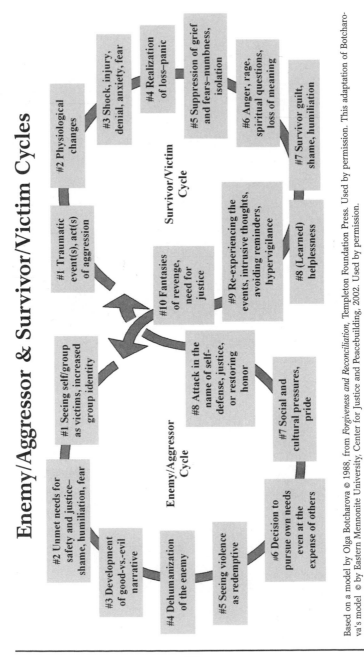

Survivor/Victim Cycle

#1 Traumatic event(s), act(s) of aggression

#2 Physiological changes

#3 Shock, injury, denial, anxiety, fear

#4 Realization of loss–panic

#5 Suppression of grief and fears–numbness, isolation

#6 Anger, rage, spiritual questions, loss of meaning

#7 Survivor guilt, shame, humiliation

#8 (Learned) helplessness

#9 Re-experiencing the events, intrusive thoughts, avoiding reminders, hypervigilance

#10 Fantasies of revenge, need for justice

Enemy/Aggressor Cycle

#1 Seeing self/group as victims, increased group identity

#2 Unmet needs for safety and justice–shame, humiliation, fear

#3 Development of good-vs.-evil narrative

#4 Dehumanization of the enemy

#5 Seeing violence as redemptive

#6 Decision to pursue own needs even at the expense of others

#7 Social and cultural pressures, pride

#8 Attack in the name of self-defense, justice, or restoring honor

Based on a model by Olga Botcharova © 1988, from *Forgiveness and Reconciliation*, Templeton Foundation Press. Used by permission. This adaptation of Botcharova's model © by Eastern Mennonite University, Center for Justice and Peacebuilding, 2002. Used by permission.

At the time they seem logical and even honorable. After all, they are familiar neural pathways! However, the second part of the model, the Enemy/Aggressor Cycle on page 38 shows how these meaning-making scripts can lead into deadly cycles of violence that can impact families, communities, and nations for generations.

This part of the model is an acting-out response. While at first glance it may seem to relate most to situations such as terrorist attacks, similar dynamics occur with those who experience natural disasters or structural violence. (See Jean Handley's story on pages 49-50.)

Although the Enemy/Aggressor Cycle follows a more predictable progression than the Survivor/Victim Cycle, few situations are neatly linear. As before, the numbers on each of the points are for ease of reference in the following explanation. The concepts were originally applied to large-group conflicts, and this will be the focus in the following discussion. However, they may also apply to individuals, as in a bitter divorce conflict.

The Enemy/Aggressor Cycle is not an inevitable response to traumatic events but it is exceedingly common. In fact, Volkan speaks of these reactions as "the rituals of large-group psychology" that come into play where there are ethnic, national, or religious conflicts, hostilities, or wars.[34] This cycle is set in motion when healing has not taken place and groups see themselves as victims who have been wronged (#1). The sense of victimhood may be from historic events, such as a chosen trauma, or from

> In people's experience, what happened centuries ago has echoes in what happened last week.
> —Douglas R. Baker[35]

a recent crisis as when the pride and identity of a previously secure group is punctured by a provocative threat or surprise attack.

Regardless of the origins, the more the security of a group is shattered or threatened, the harder the members cling to their group identify (#2). A sense of "us-vs.-them" develops or deepens and is expressed through patriotic or in-group symbols such as flags, songs, dress, food, and other customs.

Good-vs.-evil narratives

In a hyper-alert climate, groups unthinkingly adopt good-vs.-evil narratives to explain what happened and provide a sense of vindication (#3). It allows the "good" side to project their unwanted characteristics onto the enemy who is stripped of human goodness.[36] Projecting evil out onto the other shifts attention away from the "good" side's own shortcomings, their contribution to the conflict, and their own dysfunctions or internal societal ills. In essence, the "other" becomes the sacrificial scapegoat.

Leaders, media, and unreflective citizens can sustain good-vs.-evil narratives until they take on a life of their own. Such stories may become the chosen trauma around which a group organizes its collective identity. Once embedded in a culture, a chosen trauma narrative is difficult to dispel.

In this atmosphere, truth becomes the first casualty. Facts are twisted, motivations embellished, and heroes and villains created. Challenging the narrative is seen as betrayal.

When a group or nation buys into a good-vs.-evil narrative, demonizing and then dehumanizing the other easily follows (#4). Names like "terrorist," the "evil axis," or "infidel" are interwoven with descriptors like "inhuman," "insane," "animals," "barbaric." When the "other" is dehumanized and evil, then sanctity-of-life moral standards do not apply. Thus, a dangerously simplistic analysis with an equally simplistic solution gains momentum: if evil people or groups are the cause, then the the solution is to separate ourselves from them, somehow get rid of them, or even kill them.

Redemptive-violence narratives

The second common narrative pattern is the ancient narrative of redemptive violence: violence must be used to overcome violence (#5). Violence appears to have the power to make us secure, keep us free, and restore a sense of pride and honor.[37] In Lam's story, he says:

> The feeling of "chosen trauma" has engulfed whole communities and tribes. They justify acts of revenge for their victimization and identify fellow citizens as "the other" who deserve their suffering. For instance, most people felt it was justified to use "scorched-earth" military tactics because "we, too, suffered at their hands." All Northerners were labeled "anya-nya," killers who deserve to be killed. Many innocent people were killed in the cruelest way—being burnt with car tires around their necks.[38]

As Gil Bailie and others have suggested, the narrative of redemptive violence can be applied to the future, justifying violence against the "other." It can also be applied to the past, justifying and helping to explain the present.[39]

The role of leaders

Threat and security are real issues that need to be addressed by groups and nations. But when leaders and citizens alike are hypervigilant and emotions run high, it is frequently difficult to determine the true measure of threat (#6, 7). Although this may not be intentional or conscious, "malignant leaders," as Volkan calls them,[40] escalate anxiety and fear by:

- Magnifying dangers
- Blurring reality and fantasy
- Barraging the public with constant reminders of looming, unspecific potential threats
- Manipulating by withholding, distorting, or misrepresenting facts, goals, and situations
- Engaging in name-calling
- Labeling dissenting views as unpatriotic or traitorous
- Dehumanizing by using "us/them" and "good/evil" dichotomies

In traumatic circumstances, perception matters as much as the truth when it comes to group response and willingness to follow such leaders. The greater the perceived threat, the greater the group's identity or sense of nationalism becomes, and the greater the possibility that dying for one's cause or country is deemed as preferable to losing that identity. Also, the greater the perceived threat, the greater the "egoism of victimization"—that is, the tendency to become so focused and blinded by our own pain that we fail to see the pain we cause to others.[41]

Louise Diamond, co-founder of the Institute for Multi-Track Diplomacy, describes it like this:

I have watched political leaders all over the world use fear to manipulate the people. It is a common tactic, one of whose outcomes is to ensure that those in power stay in power. It plays to the lowest tones of human consciousness rather than to the highest. To keep the people hypnotical-

ly caught in a fog of fear is to keep them helpless, thereby undermining democracy and preventing the evolution of human society and spirit.[42]

Traumatized individuals, groups, and nations play out these ancient narratives as if asleep, unaware of the mythic drama that is unfolding. Regardless of whether we call this phenomenon living unconsciously, lower-mode brain function, collective denial, the lower nature, reenactment of trauma, sin, or group-think, the end result is the same: an attack against "the other" is justified in the name of self-defense, justice, security, honor, or freedom (#8).

Perceptions often matter as much as truth.

But the security we yearn, fight, and die for is rarely the long-term outcome. Violence, even within the parameters of a just war or holy war, leaves in its wake more traumatized, humiliated, hypervigilant, angry, fearful, and grieving peoples and societies. It creates more groups with a heightened sense of identity, with their own good-vs.-evil narratives, and with needs for justice and vindication. It starts more survivor/victim cycles that can morph into new enemy/aggressor cycles of violence. And so, another tit-for-tat story, like those that fill our news every day, begins anew. Lam says:

Violence was institutionalized as a response to political issues that required dialogue and understanding. The desire for revenge only perpetuated the violence.

The cycles across generations

Contrary to the popular adage, time does not heal all wounds. Unhealed trauma is passed from generation to generation in families, communities, and nations. It is *acted in* through depression, anxiety, and the effects of substance, domestic, or child abuse, and it affects family, community, and societal systems. It is *acted out* through the process we just discussed.

Succeeding generations bear the brunt of the frozen grief and acting-in and acting-out behaviors of the elders. In addition, they may be given "shared tasks" such as continuously grieving the ancestors' loss, feeling their victimization, striving for justice, or getting revenge. The common denominator in all these shared tasks is to keep the large group's memories alive. Generally these tasks cannot be effectively dealt with by the next generation, so they are passed on to yet another generation, sometimes in a changed form.[43]

> Violence often creates trauma. Trauma often leads to more violence.

How can individuals and societies avoid getting stuck in the cycle of victimhood and violence in insecure times? How do leaders—traumatized along with their citizens—provide for both short- and long-term security, yet not set in motion tit-for-tat cycles of violence?

In the next chapter, we examine a map that emerged from people who were in the abyss and are seeking a way through. It is a way that espouses neither passivity in the face of threat, nor violence as a means to security.

5.
Breaking the Cycles: The Journey to Healing and Security

If something terrible has happened to you, to those you love, it is an understandable and normal response to hate, to be bitter, to want revenge. The problem is...it will not destroy our enemies, it will destroy us. We have to find ways of acknowledging the poison and letting it go. That is a journey we need to travel.
— Fr. Michael Lapsley, SSM[44]

Part III of the Breaking the Cycles model, shown on page 47, is about finding security through trauma healing and transforming relationships. It is based on a revolutionary paradox: that we become more secure when we promote the security of our neighbors, friend and enemy alike. The ideas presented here are neither perfected nor complete. They are simply part of the quest to find a life-giving way to respond to violence and trauma.

Moving beyond fight, flight, or freeze reactions requires attention to healing body, mind, and spirit. Martha Cabrera describes the need for "affective and spiritual reconstruction" for individuals, communities, and societies that have experienced violence. Peter Levine speaks of the resilience, creativity, cooperative spirit, and sense of triumph experienced by those who heal. Paula Gutlove and others point out the importance of psychosocial healing; that is, psychological and social-support activities that help societies function in stable and healthy ways in the wake of conflict.[45]

A paradox: we become more secure when we promote the security of our friends and enemies.

At STAR, we see a hunger for ways to respond to threat that do not rely on attacking other groups. We believe we would all be more secure if even a portion of the intellectual and financial resources that now go into preparing for defending ourselves through war were devoted to societal trauma healing and training grassroots peoples and governments to respond to peril in nonviolent ways.

Background to the model

Before reading the next section, I recommend that you examine the Breaking the Cycles diagram on page 47. The inner cycle is an abbreviated combination of the victim and acting-out cycles. The broken lines suggest that it is possible to break out of these cycles at any time.

Like the other parts of the model, this two-dimensional diagram does not capture the dynamic complexity of working for lasting security and trauma healing. Also, the discussion that follows may seem to jump from the personal to the communal. This is because the personal is often communal or social and vice versa.

The "points" on the outer cycle are numbered, again, not because the process is linear but for ease of reference. The snail shape itself is metaphoric: the process may take months, years, even decades. A detailed expla-

Breaking the Cycles: The Journey to Healing and Security

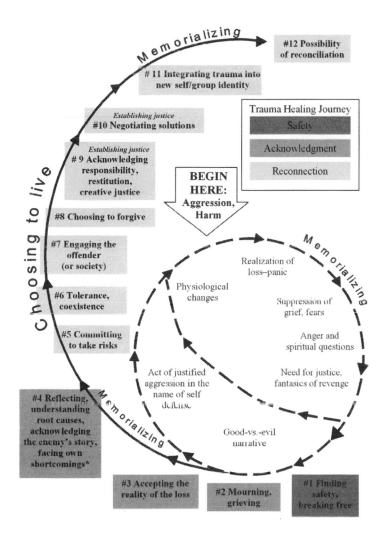

Trauma Healing Journey: Breaking the Cycles

*This does not apply in all cases, for example, child sexual abuse, where those traumatized have no responsibility for what happened.

Based on a model by Olga Botcharova © 1988, from *Forgiveness and Reconciliation*, Templeton Foundation Press. Used by permission. This adaptation of Botcharova's model © by Eastern Mennonite University, Center for Justice and Peacebuilding, 2002. Used by permission.

nation of all twelve points is beyond the scope of this book, but all fall under the three main general headings, which will be discussed: Safety, Acknowledgment, and Reconnection.[46] Other books in this *Little Book* series address parts of this cycle in more detail.[47]

This part of the model was originally constructed to describe the healing process in response to human-caused violence. Several of the points, however, are applicable to natural disasters and dealing with the issues of justice that often accompany them.

Safety: Breaking free (#1)

Safety is foundational to trauma healing. It is the best antidote to threat and fear.[48] Indeed, it is often said that safety is a precondition for healing.

But the many situations of ongoing conflict and violence in our world lead to a circular question: if healing must wait for an outbreak of security and peace, and if unhealed trauma contributes to cycles of victimhood and violence, can there be peace without healing? Can there be healing without peace?

We all know individuals who triumphed in spite of a lack of safety. Viktor Frankl experienced inner freedom, even in a concentration camp.[49] In 1999 Lam Cosmas became head of the Acholi Religious Leaders Peace Initiative, an interfaith organization of Muslim and Christian leaders committed to peacebuilding in this still-dangerous area. Countless others whose stories are not widely known have found ways to live as compassionate persons in spite of trauma, danger, or reasons to retaliate. Likewise, communities that might have responded with hatred and violence have demonstrated the ability to live nonviolently.

After Hurricane Katrina

I lost my home, community, and livelihood as a result of Hurricane Katrina. Right now I'm living in Memphis with my sister. Like many others, I don't know what I'm going to do. We're all dealing with survival: food and clothing and FEMA and food stamps.

At first I was angry at how this disaster was handled by the federal government. I wasn't angry at any one person per se, but could only think of what happened to those who were left in the city, those who were most vulnerable. Before the hurricane, many people lived under conditions of slow death. But can you imagine the shame and humiliation of being left without food, water, or medicine, in filth, watching people die, and, as far as they could perceive, without people knowing or caring? The dehumanization appeared extreme.

Then there was the environment. I knew of people who had worked and advocated for saving the wetlands and reinforcing the levees, but heard that over the last years, sewer and water funds that should have gone to strengthening the levees were misappropriated.

It took several days until I was able to recognize that I was framing what happened in us-vs.-them terms and realized that I had succumbed to a violent mindset. Of course I want to see people held accountable, but I knew that my own attitude was only contributing to the problem.

After letting go of these judgments, I began to understand that this was an opportunity to cease giving up my/our power to governments and systems, and to come back to caring for one another as a community of humans. I didn't diminish the losses, the separation of children and families, the challenge that some may now try to turn New Orleans into a white mid-

> *dle-class community. Still, it was an opportunity for ordinary citizens to come forward and rise to the occasion.*
>
> *Through this process of letting go of blaming, I came more to a place of inner peace. Grief could replace anger, and rebuilding could replace grief.*
>
> —Jean Handley

What loosens the grip of the fight, flight, and freeze response in these individuals and communities, allowing profound healing to occur in the midst of threat and insecurity? What releases them physiologically from the lower brain's instinct to act only for one's own survival?

In peacebuilding workshops in the former Yugoslavia, participants reflected on times when they were threatened and, by conventional reasoning, had "the right" to strike back. Muslims, Christians, and those of no religious faith reported remarkably similar experiences: "small secret doubts" had surfaced about the rightness of the actions they were contemplating. When they chose to follow "the still small voice" and not strike back, they realized a profound truth: the worst evil is not death; the worst evil is betraying the soul by ignoring the inner voice. As a consequence, they discovered they had lost their fear of death and experienced a significant sense of connection "with the source of spiritual power." We soar as human beings, they concluded, by "acting well in spite of threat."[50]

These experiences point to the ability of the human spirit to begin the healing processes and act in ways beyond basic survival needs, even when complete physical safety is not assured. Perhaps the traditional wisdom about safety needs to be reframed:

- What *degree* of safety?
- What *kind* of safety?

Does being grounded psychologically, socially (in a community), emotionally, and spiritually create safe spaces, even an inner space, that allows healing to begin even without complete physical safety? Does knowing our ideals and values, and what we are willing to die for,[51] provide an inner strength that pushes us beyond fear? Is "acting well in spite of threat" the key to breaking, preventing, and transcending the traumatic cycles of victimhood and violence that undermine long-term security? Do such actions surprise and throw the "enemy" off guard, creating a chink in their defensive armor—and ours? And if so, how do we promote and cultivate this ability, both individually and as societies?[52]

Some of the factors that help cultivate such a stance include:

Strategies of Trauma Healing

- Learning viable nonviolent, nonpassive alternatives to threat.
- Social support from inside and outside the trauma situation.
- A sustaining faith or spiritual practice.
- Positive leaders.
- An active willingness to move beyond victimhood or violence.
- An understanding of the trauma cycle and ideas for breaking free of it.
- Using mind-body techniques to counter hyperarousal.

Harvard physician Herbert Benson has spent decades researching ways to elicit the relaxation response in the body, which calms the automatic reactions controlled by the lower brain. These "activities" include repetitive exercise, repetitive prayer, meditation, yoga, guided imagery, mindfulness, and progressive muscle relaxation.[53] Other activities that people have found helpful include sports, massage, drumming, singing, journaling, art, and dancing.

Esther Harder, a volunteer teacher in northern Uganda, reports:

> I am using soccer as an answer to fear . . . As we boun-ce around the termite mounds, potholes, and saplings trying to score, it is much easier to feel like a normal human being. The solders are still at the sidelines, and the helicopters still hover, but during the deafening jubilation after a goal, shoulders loosen from tension and smiles brighten the dusk.[54]

Safety: The role of leaders

In times of crisis, the way community and national leaders interpret events, frame the narrative, and address needs can either inflame the situation further or bring a measure of rationality and calm in difficult times. Positive leaders serve as an "auxiliary orbitofrontal cortex" for their people; that is, they help them calm down so they can think beyond knee-jerk reactions. They lead the way through the crisis that is neither passive nor violent. Depending on the situation, this help may come from counselors, religious or political leaders, or persons with expertise in trauma and peacebuilding.

In contrast to the characteristics of "malignant leaders" noted in Chapter 4, Volkan's research has identified the following traits of positive or "reparative leaders."[55] Such leaders help their people to:

- separate fantasy from reality, and the past from the present
- evaluate and face realistic dangers and problem-solve

- learn about the humanity of enemy groups
- hold the tension of paradox
- restore ties to families, clans, and other groups that support reconnecting to reality
- value freedom of speech and consider what is moral

But what happens when the leaders themselves are impacted by traumatic events or are caught up in narrow ethnic or nationalist thinking? Then they, too, would benefit from getting advice and counsel from persons or groups outside the circle of impact to help them think through responses to threat beyond fight, flight, or freeze.

In large-group traumas when even national leaders are affected, allies of the affected country or organizations such as NATO, the African Union (AU), the Association of South East Asian Nations (ASEAN,) or the Organization of American States (OAS), or the United Nations (UN) could fill this function.

Acknowledgment: Mourning, grieving our own story, and naming fears (#2-3)

Mourning and grieving are essential for finding healing and breaking the cycles. Acknowledging and telling the story counteracts the isolation, silence, fear, shame, or "unspeakable" horror. It allows the frozen sadness to melt. There are differences of opinion at to how much detail is needed for healing and whether delving too deeply into the memory or experience is necessary—or even harmful. However, there is agreement that storytelling includes the integration of both facts and emotions.

Judith Herman stresses the need to open up gradually to ensure that the memories and feelings do not plunge us into hyperarousal again.[56] Levine uses the term "renegotiation" to describe a measured undulation between re-leasing the energy blockages of the body, feeling the ac-companying emotions, and using our intellects to keep us from moving too fast and being overwhelmed.[57] He offers practical and caring guidance for how to tell stories in ways that do not deepen the trauma.[58] Many traditional cultures have or had rituals and ceremonies that allowed for a similar process to happen in a community setting.

Various forms of expression can be used: art, music, dance, drama, writing, prayer, meditation, cultural ritu-als, and cleansing ceremonies. Techniques such as massage and other forms of body and energy work can be utilized or taught in community settings. Eye Movement De-sensitization and Reprocessing[59] (EMDR), Thought Field Therapy[60] (TFT), and So-matic Experiencing[61] can be employed. Memorials can provide a physical place to grieve, a symbolic expression of loss, and the comfort that our loved ones will not be unacknowledged or forgotten.

> Acknowl-edgment opens the way to post-traumatic growth.

When all of the story is acknowledged and mourned—the valor, heroism, sacrifice, pain, fear, resilience, be-trayals, humiliations, shortcomings, atrocities, and guilt—then shame and humiliation can be shed, forgiveness sought, courage celebrated, and reenactment ended.

Martha Cabrera observes that when her people began to reconstruct, talk about, reflect on, and assume their personal and national history, a fundamental change oc-curred. Despite everything that happened, they found meaning and significance in what they had lived through and in what they became. This helped them move for-ward in positive ways.[62]

Acknowledgment and the subsequent grieving and mourning help us accept that life will never be the same. However, facing the possibility of a "new normal" can bring up a host of fears about the future, fears that must be identified and realistically addressed. Otherwise, individuals or groups remain easily susceptible to triggers that can throw them back into the victim or aggressor cycles. Facing the past, the reality of the present, and the challenges in the future open the way for post-traumatic growth.

Acknowledgment: Recognizing that "the other" has a story (#4)

The universal cry, "Why me?" or "Why us?" reflects the longing to find reason and meaning in difficult life events. Yet continually asking these often-unanswerable questions keeps us stuck. Together with suppressed fears, these questions provoke the greatest anger at everything and everyone associated with the perpetrator.[63] To restore the ability to think rationally, the question needs to be reframed to "Why them? Why did they do it, and why did they do it to us?"[64] This opens the way to search for root causes and to acknowledge that the other, the enemy, also has a story.

"Why them?" questions require more than sound-byte answers. Father Michael Lapsley, who lost both hands and sight in one eye from a letter bomb mailed to him while he was working to end apartheid in South Africa, identifies three questions individuals and groups must reflect on if they are to end violence and find healing:[65]

- What was done to me/us?
- What did I/we do to others?
- What did I/we fail to do?

(There are some situations for which these are inappropriate questions: for example, in cases of child abuse or genocide. Yet even adults who are on a healing journey to recover from childhood abuse may find these questions useful in reflecting on the choices they are making *as adults* in response to the abuse.)

Serious reflection on these questions requires a willingness to challenge our basic beliefs about who we are. It requires knowledge of our own history as well as the history of the other, the enemy. We may need to delve into decades, even centuries, of history to understand present events. We may never be able to fully understand.

Seeking to understand root causes does *not* mean condoning what happened. In the aftermath of 9-11, "Why us?" questions soon were intermingled with "Why do they hate us?" This was a cry for answers, not agreement with the attack.

It is not easy or comfortable to look at the history of those who hurt us. What often emerges is that our enemy acted out of the anger, fear, and even the helplessness of being wronged or victimized—sometimes by us or by our group. This in no way excuses them of responsibility for crimes or atrocities. They are responsible for the way they chose to respond to these historic events, just as we are responsible for our actions and reactions when our security is threatened or when we are attacked or harmed. But learning the history opens our eyes to the present context and to the complexity of life. It makes us aware that who is named as victim or aggressor depends upon the segment of history we are studying and from whose side we are viewing the story. It leads to the ability to openly acknowledge hypocrisy and the collective transgressions of our own people.[60]

Marie shares from her story:

I said to myself, "Marie, you are really angry." It was cellular, a physical, raw, rage. And then I realized this is the same level of rage that led those guys to fly the planes into buildings—helpless, desperate to make a change in conditions. Wow! I knew I had to engage this post-9-11 journey until it was done. I really needed to understand as much as I could about the nuts and bolts of what created this situation, and what was so painful for other people that this was the best they could do to express their needs. And I'm still not done.

Reflecting on Fr. Lapsley's questions, then, opens a space within us as individuals or groups to see our own shadows, shortcomings, and failings. It brings us face-to-face with our own prejudices and biases. It begins the process of rehumanizing the demonized enemy. And it shatters simplistic, polarizing good-vs.-evil narratives.

This process can take months or even years. But as we learn more about the other, anger and hate begin to be replaced by understanding and even compassion, a sense of affinity, and humility.[68] We may find ourselves willing to take risks with policy and action unimaginable only a short time before.

> Today's aggressors are often yesterday's victims.
> —Olga Botcharova[67]

Reconnection: Recognizing interdependence, taking risks (#5-7)

With an understanding of history comes an awareness of our interconnectedness and interdependence as human beings and nations. With this awareness comes an openness to risk contact with the other. Individuals, communities, or groups must decide what level of risk they are ready to take on. A commitment to risk is not an injunction to put oneself in harm's way or to be in an abusive situation. When former enemies meet, strong emotions can be retriggered and cause old memories and emotions to come flooding back.

Trauma researcher Bessel van der Kolk says that although studies have not been conducted with groups in conflict, he believes that body practices such as *gui gong* and yoga would help them engage constructively.[69] Patricia Mathes Cane has taught mind-body exercises—massage, *tai chi*, singing, acupuncture, and others that elicit the relaxation response—to villagers, professionals, political prisoners, heath workers, and groups in conflict areas in many parts of the world.[70] These workouts calm the body and help brain function to remain integrated.

How this engagement with the other actually takes place varies with each situation. When the harm is personal, one-on-one meetings can take place either alone or with a third-party facilitator. In some cultures, exchanges take place through intermediaries or through community processes.

At a social level, the Truth and Reconciliation Commission in South Africa provided a way for victims to tell their "truths" and to find answers to questions in a public meeting. In some cases, victims also were able to listen to the testimony of perpetrators. Although only a few cases allowed for direct encounters between the two parties, the hearings often did address important needs and served to humanize "the other."

Ordinary citizens can meet the other side in situations of conflict through a variety of ways. Some programs bring together young people from both sides of a conflict to work on projects. A mountain retreat in Caux, Switzerland, has provided an unofficial meeting place for adversaries since World War II. A sewing class was formed for women on opposite sides of the conflict in the Sudan. A Brooklyn, New York, school teacher and his class began an e-mail correspondence with an Iraqi school teacher and his students in Fallujah when that city was being bombarded by the U.S. in 2004.

Sometimes meeting the offender is impossible. After 9-11, the hijackers of the planes were dead, and meeting with other al-Qaida members was not an option. So several people who lost family members formed a group called "September 11 Families for Peaceful Tomorrows."[71] Some traveled to Afghanistan and others to Iraq to share stories and grief with civilians there who had also lost family members in the war on terror. They continue as an advocacy group promoting policies of nonviolence, understanding, and engagement in situations of conflict.

When the harm is caused by neighbors, it can be especially difficult to go beyond a surface level or reach levels of security and safety. This is a long process aided by knowing the history of each other, by getting outside help, and by understanding how individual and collective memory are shaped by both facts and perception.[73] The purpose of meeting together is to bring understand-

> The traumatized say, "Never again." And they do whatever it takes to keep themselves and their group safe. The traumawise[72] say, "Never again—to me, to us, or to anyone else." And they work to make the world a safe place for everyone.

ing, not to use suffering as a weapon against each other.[74]

When we choose to act in new ways, the brain forms new neural pathways.

As we have seen, when we choose to act in new ways, the brain literally forms new neural pathways. Healthy encounters contradict the helplessness and paralysis of traumatizing events. They contradict the habitual way of responding to stressful triggers that further weaken feelings of control and connection.[75] The rewards are palpable. Something powerful happens when people meet face to face. "In meeting each other, we discover that we're really part of the same family that somehow has got broken up," says the Rev. Kenneth Newell of Northern Ireland.[76]

From such encounters can grow a shared sense of responsibility to reshape the future and to restore harmony at a personal, community, emotional, social, and spiritual level. Aided by grace, creative ideas start to flow. We feel more resilient, and others are drawn into the process. Our emotions, which used to pull us down, begin to raise us up.[77]

Lam states:

Yes, there are still rebels in the bush, and the area is still insecure. They just ambushed one of our priests and three people died. They just chopped off the fingers of a woman. But some came out of the bush . . . and they are being integrated back into the community. Those rebels— they are our former enemy. But I am meeting with their leaders and helping them with income-generation projects and organization and bookkeeping. One day the chairman of the group came to me and said, "I hear you are doing workshops for the community on peace. Don't you think we need a workshop on peace?" So I will do a workshop for them. We will focus on human relationships. It will help their reintegration process.

Reconnection: Choosing the path to forgiving (#8)

To some, forgiving is an obscene word in the wake of profound human wrongdoing and evil. Indeed, if it is defined as forgetting, or equated with foregoing the quest for justice, the effort to forgive may do more harm than good. If it is experienced as a moral or religious duty than a hopeful possibility, it may be more of a burden than a gift.

Forgiving is especially difficult when violence is continuing or the sense of hurt still exists and has not been honored or acknowledged. But when one has witnessed or experienced bitterness that can consume individuals or groups as they spin in cycles of victimhood and violence, it is evident that humans need a loftier goal than punishment or revenge, even in the face of great suffering.[78]

Forgiveness is NOT forgetting or foregoing justice.

Forgiving offers a release from the burden of bitterness. It does not mean giving up the quest for justice, but letting go of the cycles of revenge and retribution to pursue a justice in a way that is restorative to victims and aggressors alike, and may lay the groundwork for reconciliation.

However, if we have done the hard work of rehumanizing the other by acknowledging their story, forgiving takes on new meaning and may not be a simple one-way process. As we have seen, the designation of "victim" and "aggressor" often depends on the particular slice of history we are viewing. Therefore, reciprocal acts of acknowledgment, remorse, repentance, and forgiveness are appropriate in many cases. For example, religious leaders in both Britain and Ireland have expressed remorse and asked forgiveness of the other.[79]

Even so, choosing the path toward forgiving can be difficult. Some things can never be undone or restored. The ability to continue the process is a gift from God. As such, it contains elements of grace and mystery and is not the exclusive domain of any particular religion or group.

Forgiving is a process that is made easier if our hurt is acknowledged by others, especially by the "enemy." Yet if we link our conditions for forgiving to the responses of those who hurt us, we stay forever in their power. Regardless of their actions or response, we choose whether or not to walk the journey of forgiving.

In forgiving, the intrapersonal, interpersonal, and communal are intertwined in complex ways. What this means and how it is done on a group or societal/national level is particularly challenging. Donald Shriver describes forgiveness in a political context as "an act that joins moral truth, forbearance, empathy, and commitment to repair a fractured human relationship."[81]

The Woodstock Center of Georgetown University has held a series of meetings looking at how forgiveness is practiced at national levels. The participants agreed that

> True forgiveness is achieved in community . . . It is history working itself out as grace, and it can be accomplished only in truth. That truth, however, is not mere knowledge. It is acknowledgment. It is a coming to terms with and it is a labor.
>
> —Hanah Arendt[80]

a culture of forgiveness must be built through actions at the personal, cultural, and political levels. National and civil-society leaders in positions of symbolic authority play a critical role in moving the society in a direction of forgiveness and creating openness for creative reconciliation later.[82] Truth and reconciliation commissions, created in Sierra Leone, El Salvador, South Africa, and other places, are important steps in this direction.

Forgiving also may involve restitution. As we become aware of how we have wronged others, we recognize our need to take responsibility to repair as much as we can. In this way, we prepare to live into a future that will be different from the past. This is both an individual and collective responsibility.

Reconnection: Seeking justice (#9-10)

In a perfect world, justice would begin with the offenders—whether individuals, groups, or governments—admitting guilt, apologizing publicly, offering compensation, and making sure that the events do not happen again.

But the world is not perfect. Neither is justice. Nor are victims' expectations always clear or realistic. Often there is an unspoken assumption that justice will restore a sense of normalcy and relieve the pain. Sometimes it does, but often it does not. Sometimes justice can satisfy an abstract sense of what is right, while failing to help those who have been harmed to heal or break out of the cycles. Someone has said, "The fight for justice can make people ugly. That is, your motive in fighting for justice can be as ugly as the thing that you're seeking to fight."[83]

This is not to suggest that individuals and groups should not seek justice. Rather, it is an acknowledgment that the needs that trauma and violence create are complex, and there are limits to the healing the justice system can provide. Ideally, it serves the common good and helps to create order. But it alone cannot heal.

The usual approach to justice in today's world is the legal or criminal-justice approach, enshrined in national systems and international tribunals. This justice approach tends to be organized around three questions:

1. What law was broken?
2. Who did it?
3. What do the law-breakers deserve?

What they are seen to deserve, usually, is some form of punishment.

This criminal-justice approach often serves an important role in identifying wrongdoers and denouncing wrongdoing. At its best, it is designed to safeguard human rights and provide an orderly justice process. It has an important role to play but unfortunately often does little to address the needs of victims or aid in healing. Preoccupied with making sure wrongdoers get what they deserve, it often does little to encourage offenders to understand what they did or to take real responsibility for it. And often its adversarial style exacerbates conflicts and wounds in society more than it heals.

To address the needs that this criminal justice approach does not meet, a *restorative-justice* concept and movement is rapidly spreading throughout the world. Restorative justice focuses on harms done and offers a needs-based understanding of justice that attends to the needs and obligations of all involved. Restorative justice is organized around the following guiding questions:[84]

- Who has been hurt?
- What are their needs?

- Whose obligations are they?
- What are the causes?
- Who has a stake in the situation?
- What process can include all involved in addressing needs and obligations and finding a solution?

The question "Who has been hurt?" acknowledges that those victimized must be central, but also that harm goes beyond direct victims. Family, friends, the community, and society as a whole can be hurt. The offender, too, may be among those who were hurt, demonstrating again the complexity of the labels "victim" and "offender."

Restorative justice also focuses on accountability, i.e. on the obligations involved in the hurt, and on the importance of trying to right the wrongs as much as possible. It also seeks to involve those impacted by the wrongdoing in the solution to it.[85] In some circumstances, it may offer an encounter between victims and offenders.

Healing justice approaches

- Restorative justice
- Transformative justice
- Creative justice

When the act(s) resulted—even in part—from unhealthy relationships or social or political structures, the search for justice requires us to look behind individual acts to the systemic. *Transformative justice* asks:

- What circumstances and structures permitted or encouraged this?
- What structural similarities exist between this and other similar acts or incidents?

- What measures can be taken to change these structures and circumstances to reduce future occurrences?

Resolution, then, involves working to change larger social and political systems to help prevent recurrence of the harm.[86]

> When attempts at justice fall short, some look to *creative justice.*

The concepts of restorative justice and transformative justice are embedded in Robert Joseph's writing on reconciliatory justice, which is being applied to address and settle land seizure and other injustices against indigenous peoples. Joseph describes reconciliatory justice as "a dispute-resolution concept, ideal, process, and strategy for overcoming the politics of denial and for appropriately resolving some . . . post-settlement challenges, issues, and tensions."[87]

Transitional justice is a way of assisting societies that have been through repressive rule or armed conflict to find ways that hold accountable those responsible for past mass atrocity or human-rights abuses. Transitional justice may include judicial and nonjudicial responses such as prosecuting individual perpetrators, paying reparations to victims of state-sponsored violence, establishing truth-seeking initiatives about past abuse, and reforming institutions like the police and the courts. As such, it can be either restorative or punative.

No matter what the approach, sincere attempts at justice can fall short. Aggressors may never be caught or may be unavailable. Counts, tribunals, and truth commissions do not satisfy all. If the damage was caused by organized crime or by a government, impunity may rule the day. Things often cannot be "made right."

No easy answers exist. Indeed, perhaps no answers exist. But some have taken a proactive route of what Wilma Derksen has called *creative justice*.[88] This may be approached through symbolic acts, such as the memorial created by Wilma's community in memory of her murdered daughter.

Or the energy of unrequited justice may be transferred into working to prevent such harm from happening again. For example, a woman whose child was killed by a drunk driver started Mothers Against Drunk Driving (MADD). The September 11 Families for Peaceful Tomorrows will never have the satisfaction of traditional justice, but they do have the satisfaction of working toward a world where hate and revenge do not have the final word. Torture survivors have formed the Torture Abolition and Survivors Support Coalition International (TASSC) and are putting their energy into ending torture through education, lobbying governments, and starting support groups for survivors.

> Ideally, justice deals with the past so that we can move into the future.

The work for seeking formal justice may go on. But through creative justice, one's energy, future, and gifts are not held hostage to the traumatic injustice or the outcome of a legal ruling.

Ideally, then, justice deals with the past, setting things as right as is possible, so that we can move into the future. It may open the way for joint planning with former adversaries. Projects such as writing a common history together can be initiated. A primary goal is assuring human security and dignity for all. This is possible if both sides can answer the question, "What would make a political culture and a political system that would meet the deepest needs of your (former) opponents?"[89]

Reconnection: Possibility of reconciliation (#10-11)

Reconciliation is not an event, something that happens at a precise moment. Rather, it is the result of the labor and grace of the healing journey just described. Achieving "as much justice as possible"[90] and forgiving are essential keys, but they do not guarantee reconciliation. When reconciliation happens, however, it is evident in the transformation of attitudes, beliefs, and behaviors toward former enemies and offenders. Trauma and suffering are neither forgotten nor excused, but better understood and integrated into a new self or group identity. A sense of safety and well-being replaces fear.

Marie says:

> This doesn't go away; it's not over. In a sense this is a beginning. I can almost honestly say the word "gift." This is an existential, full-on call from the deepest depths of what we call God to really get real about what is important, what is truth, what is life, not just in an understanding way, but in a way that changes how I live and demands impeccability and life-long commitment.

The transformation of trauma into hope for the future by breaking cycles of victimhood and violence is a long journey. It involves work on multiple dimensions: the spiritual, the emotional, the intellectual, the physical—and this on the communal as well as the personal levels.

In the past chapters we looked at some of the causes and manifestations of trauma and suggested some ways to break free from traumas we have experienced. In the next chapter, we look at ways we might have dealt differently with the traumatic events of the past. We then explore a few ways to prepare for traumatic events that may lie ahead.

6.
What If?
9-11 and
Breaking the Cycles

When I was a little girl, my sisters and I played "house" with our dolls as our children, our imaginary husbands, and a running verbal narrative. The story line would flow with one of us picking up where the other left off as we and our dolls acted out the imagined events. Occasionally, the tale spun off in a direction we didn't like. So one of us would simply say, "Let's erase that." Sometimes we paused momentarily for a bit of negotiation. But usually, without missing a beat, the narrator returned to an earlier junction of the story and we played out a different ending.

If only real life were so simple. Alas, the magic of "erase that" belongs to childhood. Wishful thinking and "what-if" questions keep us stuck if they are used to criticize, gripe, or remain in the past. But "what if" can also help us imagine a different future—and even the present. So, let's go back to September 11, 2001 and imagine—what if?[91]

What if in the awful days after 9-11, our U.S. leaders—the president, our governors, mayors, clergy, and health professionals—had normalized our feelings of anger, bewilderment, humiliation, horror, and the desire for justice and vindication as common trauma reactions? *What if* they stated clearly that, although these low-mode reactions are normal, they should not determine the response.

What if these heinous acts were named a crime rather than an act of war? *What if* we had then asked a sympathetic international community for cooperation and help in dismantling terrorist networks, bringing them to justice, and interrupting the financial support systems that feed them?[92]

What if our leaders had known that their own trauma reactions to an attack happening on their watch could affect their judgment? *What if* they had displayed a greatness born of humility by asking our allies to help formulate a response?

What if we were encouraged to reach out to our Muslim or immigrant neighbors with random acts of kindness? *What if* cities and towns encouraged citizens to channel their trauma energy into organized hikes, dances, soccer games, tennis and golf tournaments, walks, races, and car washes to raise money for victims and survivors of violence worldwide?

What if national days of mourning were called for the purpose of being silent together, in prayer and meditation, so that we could listen for guidance and wisdom to discern a nonconventional response to the nonconventional act of flying planes into buildings?[93] *What if* the rest of the world were invited to join us in that discernment?

What if, in response to the question, "Why do they hate us?" our government had invited universities, journalists, television networks, filmmakers, and artists to produce programs to help us understand the relevant history? *What if* they had interviewed ordinary people and leaders from the Middle East and elsewhere about what their lives are like on a day-to-day basis; how they have been impacted, positively and negatively by the U.S., and what they think led to 9-11?

What if, in the study and exploration of root causes, we had discovered that for a long time real people around the globe have not only benefited from the generosity of the U.S., but also have been harmed and even killed because of our policies? Would such a discovery have allowed us to reject good-vs.-evil narratives and redemptive-violence solutions as simplistic and dangerous?

What if, with the encouragement and support of our leaders, average citizens—including the 82 percent of U.S. citizens who have never traveled abroad—participated in exchange visits, work camps, and seminars for the purpose of learning how the lives of U.S. citizens are intertwined with the lives of citizens in the rest of the world.

What if we said to each other, "We're sorry. Never again should policies or acts of terror happen—to you, to us, to anyone else." *What if,* from the grassroots to the highest levels of government, we began to address the political and economic needs and wrongs of the world?

What if even a fraction of the money spent on the war on terror were used to equip health clinics, schools, and job training centers in our country and around the world?

What if war doesn't stop terrorism?

What if it's not too late to take steps in another direction?

7.
How Then
Shall We Live?

The earth is too small a planet, and we too briefly visitors upon it, for anything to matter more than the struggle for peace.
— Coleman McCarthy[94]

If we want to leave a better world for our children, the question that faces us is this: "How then shall we live?" Following are six suggestions:

1. Recognize ourselves as leaders.

Each of us has a sphere of influence, be it as small as a family unit or as large as a nation. We can begin conversations with others about trauma and educate about tit-for-tat cycles of victimhood and violence that produce trauma and undermine security. We can speak out against polices that inflame such cycles in our communities and nations.

The figure on page 74 emerged from the STAR seminars. It identifies entry points for beginning discussions, depending on the focus or receptivity of the community or group in which we work. We may enter through work in trauma, peacebuilding, justice, human security, or spirituality. No matter what our beginning point, if the goal is building healthy and secure societies, the discussion eventually encompasses all points of the star.

STAR Model

Trauma Healing

Peacebuilding

Healthy Society

Justice

Human Security

Spirituality

2. Challenge our own faith communities to live up to the highest ideals.

In a world where worldviews and values clash, religious leaders and people of faith have a key role to play. They can get to know each other across religious lines to monitor and counteract ethnic and religious rumors and aggression. But beyond that, people of faith have the responsibility to challenge and confront those within our own religious tradition who preach hate or use our scriptures to sanction atrocities, bigotry, and aggression.[95]

3.Prevent trauma by learning to wage peace.

Working for peace is trauma prevention. Yet it is not enough to say we are against violence or war and then sit passively by. We must learn about and articulate viable options in the public forum that promote long-term nonviolent responses to conflicts and short-term responses to immediate crises. This means studying how to wage peace with the same intensity that we now study how to wage war. [96]

Nonviolent responses to conflict and threat require training as well as anticipation and preparation for a variety of scenarios. For example:

- When activists in the Ukraine suspected that the 2004 election results might be rigged, they developed a nonviolent strategy to challenge the results. In advance they gathered tents, bottled water, blankets, and other necessities that would allow sustained mass protests.
- In the build-up to the 2003 U.S.-led invasion of Iraq, the *Sojourners* community of Washington D.C. circulated a 10-point plan on how to defeat Saddam Hussein nonviolently. They encouraged churches to insert it into their bulletins, posted it on their website, and spoke about it in public venues. Obviously, it didn't stop the war. But it raised the consciousness of ordinary citizens that there are viable alternatives to all-or-nothing thinking about difficult situations.

More and more we are seeing that groups who could have resorted to violence are instead using "a force more powerful;"[97] that is, nonviolent action for social change, social defense, or third-party intervention.[98] Examples are the thousands of Serbians whose nonviolent struggle in 2000 overthrew the dictator Milosevic; the communities who defend their streets against drug trafficking by taking over the dealer's favorite spots in the neighborhood; or crowds of ordinary people who stood between two forces moving toward confrontation in the Philippines during the last days of the dictator Marcos.[99]

4.Work at both the personal and the communal/ structural levels.

Healing and peace must happen on both personal and communal levels. At a personal level, when we renegotiate the traumas of our own lives and experience healing, we can go into the world as healers, aware of our own strengths and vulnerabilities.

However, if we maintain that changing hearts and minds one by one is the only worthy work in the world, we risk ignoring the millions who suffer now. Imagine that you are a parent in a refugee camp cradling your starving child, and someone tells you that change will come only after those involved in creating your plight are convinced, softened, or converted in their hearts.

Martin Luther King, Jr. said that the law could not make a man love him, but it could stop that person "from lynching me." The personal and the social/structural are connected. Working only with one is not enough. Both are practical, spiritual endeavors, and both are to be honored and worked at simultaneously.

5. Be informed.

While it is important for people everywhere to be informed, this section addresses U.S. citizens in particular.

A London-based British Broadcasting Company (BBC) news-show host once asked their Washington correspondent why so many people in the U.S. support policies that much of the rest of the world finds disturbing and misguided. The reporter replied, "Because the U.S. is dangerously isolated."[100]

Isolated? In an age of unprecedented access to news and information from around the globe? But the reality is that many mainstream U.S. news sources are more entertainment and opinion than substance. International news is given sparse coverage in comparison to other Western democracies. Compare, for example, the news on CNN International with that of CNN U.S. International stories and viewpoints that do not fit the popularly-held image of the U.S. as good and benevolent are labeled "leftist" and "liberal" or are not reported. Criticism of our country from overseas is dismissed as "jealousy." No wonder that when 9-11 happened, a dominant and genuine question was, "Why do they hate us?"

Not infrequently, international participants at STAR voice the sentiment that they should be allowed to vote in U.S. elections. Why? Because their country's politics, their trauma, and their futures are so intertwined with and impacted by U.S. foreign policy. Yet many U.S. citizens would be horrified to know of the policies carried out in our name around the world, no matter which party is in the White House.

Information is power. A successful democracy depends on an informed populace. The BBC reporter is right. Hard as it is to hear, many of us in the United States are isolated—by our own free choice.

6. Remember that we are not alone.

Breaking destructive cycles through acting well in spite of threat is spiritual work of the deepest sort. This is not a solitary journey; we need to be connected to communities of like-minded people as we act, listen, and learn in new ways. Together we find sustenance for the long journey from the Source of Life, who has promised that light overcomes darkness, that we do not walk alone, and that a peace beyond our fears sustains us as we commit to living in healing, life-affirming ways.

How then will we live, beginning today?

Appendix:
Key Elements in
Breaking the Cycle

1. A sense of **safety** is important. When physical safety is impossible, other factors can take its place, including:
   - A decision to act well in spite of threat
   - Spiritual and psychological grounding
   - The support of others
   - Reflective leaders

2. **Acknowledgment** can lay the basis for post-traumatic growth.
   *Acknowledgment directed toward **ourselves** includes:*
   - Mourning and grieving
   - Telling the story
   - Exercises to "renegotiate" the traumatic energy
   - Naming fears
   - Expressing shame as well as honor, failings as well as strengths

   *Acknowledgment directed toward **others** includes:*
   - Seeking to understand causes (answering the question, "Why them?")
   - Attempting to see ourselves as the other sees us
   - Resisting the impulse to dehumanize and demonize the other

3. Efforts to **reconnect** with ourselves and others are the next steps. These include:
   - A sense of the interconnectedness and interrelatedness of all
   - A willingness to risk contact with the "other"
   - The possibility of forgiveness
   - A search for justice that restores and heals
   - An openness to eventual reconciliation

Endnotes

1 See *Why Marriages Succeed or Fail* (New York: Simon and Schuster, 1994) pp. 176-77.

2 The original model is presented in Olga Botcharova, "Implementation of Track Two Diplomacy" in *Forgiveness and Reconciliation*, eds. Raymond G. Helmick and Rodney L. Petersen (Radnor, PA: Templeton Foundation Press, 2001).

3 See William G. Cunningham, "Terrorism Definitions and Typologies" in *Terrorism: Concepts, Causes, and Conflict Resolution* p. 9. George Mason University. See http://www.au.af.mil/au/awc/awcgate/dtra/terrorism concepts.pdf.

4 See John Lancaster, "In Sri Lanka, A Frustrating Limbo: Rules Leave Tsunami Survivors Unable to Rebuild Lives," *The Washington Post*, March 8. 2005, p. 1.

5 The people and stories used throughout the book are true except for Jinnah and, later, Kadzu, who are composites of people I knew in Bangladesh and Kenya.

6 See Derek Summerfield, "Addressing Human Response to War and Atrocity," in *Beyond Trauma: Cultural and Societal Dynamics*, eds. Rolf J. Kebler, Charles R. Figley, Berthold P.R. Gersons (New York: Plenum Press, 1995) pp. 19-20.

7 See "Living and Surviving in a Multiply Wounded Country" at http://www.uni-klu.ac.at/ ~ hstockha/neu/html/cabreracruz.htm.

8 See Summerfield, "Addressing Human Response," p. 12.

9 For quote from Maria Yellow Horse Brave Heart, see Edna Steinman, "Native Americans Suffer from 'Historical Trauma' Researcher Says," in United Methodist News Service, July 27, 2005, at http://umns.umc.org.

10 See *Perpetration-Induced Traumatic Stress: The Psychological Consequence of Killing* (Westport, CT: Praeger Publisher, 2002). MacNair uses the term "perpetration-induced traumatic stress." I pre-

fer calling it "participation-induced traumatic stress" especially for harm caused in the line of duty.

11 A study at the University of California, Los Angeles, suggests that women produce the hormone oxytocin in response to stress. It creates a "tend-and befriend" response which counteracts fight-or-flight as she cares for her children and turns toward other women. See S.E. Taylor, et al., "Female Responses to Stress: Tend and Befriend, Not Fight or Flight," in *Psychological Review* 107, no. 3 (2000): 411-29.

12 See Peter A. Levine with Ann Frederick, *Waking the Tiger—Healing Trauma: The Innate Capacity to Transform Overwhelming Experiences* (Berkeley: North Atlantic Books, 1997) pp.19-39.

13 Ibid.

14 See Daniel J. Siegel, "The Brain in the Palm of Your Hand," in *Psychotherapy Networker* 26 (September/October 2002): 33.

15 Siegel describes this in "An Interpersonal Neurobiology of Psychotherapy" in *Healing Trauma: Attachment, Mind, Body, and Brain*, eds. Marion F. Solomon and Daniel J. Siegel (New York: W.W. Norton and Co., 2003) p. 22. See also Siegel and Mary Hartzell, *Parenting From the Inside Out: How a Deeper Self-Understanding Can Help You Raise Children Who Thrive* (New York: Penguin, 2003) p.174.

16 Ibid.

17 Howard Zehr, *Transcending: Reflections of Crime Victims* (Intercourse, PA: Good Books, 2001) pp. 186-197.

18 See Kebler, Figley, and Gersons in the Epilogue to *Beyond Trauma*, p. 302.

19 See *Trauma and Recovery* (New York: Basic Books, 1992) p. 158.

20 See Cabrera at http://www.uni-klu.ac.at/~hstockha/neu/html/cabreracruz.htm.

21 See "Training to Help Traumatized Populations," United States Institute of Peace, *Special Report* 79, at www.usip.org/pubs/specialreports/sr79.html.

22 Ibid.

Endnotes

23 Ibid.

24 Ibid. See also Vamik Volkan, *Blind Trust: Large Groups and Their Leaders in Times of Crisis and Terror* (Charlottesville, VA: Pitchstone Publishing, 2004).

25 See *Forgive for Good* (San Francisco: HarperCollins, 2002).

26 See *Diagnostic and Statistical Manual of Mental Disorders,* 4th ed. (Washington DC: American Psychiatric Association, 1994).

27 See Levine, *Waking the Tiger,* p.176.

28 See Cabrera at http://www.uni-klu.ac.at/~hstockha/neu/html/cabreracruz.htm.

29 See Vamik Volkan in the *Foreword to Cyprus: War and Adaptation: A Psychoanalytic History of Two Ethnic Groups in Conflict* (Charlottesville, VA: University of Virginia Press, 1979), pp ix-xxi.

30 Ibid.

31 See Clea Koff, *The Bone Woman: A Forensic Anthropologist's Search for Truth in the Mass Graves of Rwanda, Bosnia, Croatia, and Kosovo* (New York: Random, 2004). Koff tells of a lobbying group for families of the missing in Croatia, who demonstrated against plans to excavate/exhume mass graves in one area. They feared the bodies of their loved ones would be found and they wanted to keep hope alive.

32 See *Ambiguous Loss: Learning to Live with Unresolved Grief* (Cambridge, MA: Harvard University Press, 1999).

33 The enemy/aggressor cycle diagram and discussion are based on Enemy System Theory, Human Need Theory, and the writings of Vamik Volkan, Joseph Montville, Walter Wink, John E. Mack, Olga Botcharova, and others.

34 See "Post Traumatic States: Beyond Individual PTSD in Societies Ravaged by Ethnic Conflict" in *Psychosocial Healing: A Guide for Practitioners,* eds. Paula Gutlove and Gordon Thompson (Cambridge, MA: Institute for Resource and Security Studies, 2003) p. 81.

35 See "Forgiveness in Conflict Resolution: Reality and Utility, The Northern Ireland Experience" (paper presented at the Woodstock Theological Center Colloquium at Georgetown University, June 18, 1997) p.54.

36 See Botcharova, "Implementation of Track Two Diplomacy," p. 293.

37 See Walter Wink, *The Powers That Be: Theology for a New Millennium* (New York: Galilee, 1998) p. 91.

38 See Lam Oryen Cosmas, "Breaking the Cycle of Violence" in Mennonite Central Committee *Peace Office Newsletter* 34 (April-June 2004).

39 See *Violence Unveiled: Humanity at the Crossroads* (New York: Crossroad, 1995).

40 Volkan quoted in "Blind Trust—Author: Leaders' Actions in Crisis Impel Conflict, Peace" by Betty Booker, *Richmond Dispatch,* October 4, 2004, p E. See also Vamik Volkan, *Blind Trust: Large Groups and Their Leaders in Times of Crisis and Terror* (Charlottesville, VA: Pitchstone Publishing, 2004).

41 Ibid.

42 See http://www.imtd.org

43 See Volkan, "Post Traumatic States."

44 From a sermon preached at Cathedral of St. John the Divine, New York City, May 5, 2002. See http://www.healingofmemoires.co.za.

45 See Gutlove and Thompson, *Psychosocial Healing*.

46 Judith Lewis Herman in *Trauma and Recovery* uses the categories of safety, remembering and mourning, and reconnection. Gutlove and Thompson in *Psychosocial Healing* use the categories of safety, acknowledgment, and reconnection.

47 See Howard Zehr, *The Little Book of Restorative Justice* (Intercourse, PA: Good Books, 2002) and Lisa Schirch, *The Little Book of Strategic Peacebuilding* (Intercourse, PA: Good Books, 2004).

48 A study in the former Yugoslavia demonstrated that providing a safe physical and psychological space for rebuilding old social contacts and meeting new people helped more than any other type of psychological intervention or therapy. See Gutlove and Thompson, *Psychosocial Healing,* p 14.

49 See *Man's Search for Meaning* (New York: Pocket Books, 1997).

50 See Botcharova, "Implementation of Track Two Diplomacy" pp. 295-296.

51 Often the causes we would die for are also the same ones for which we are willing to kill. Here we speak of being willing to die *but not kill* for a cause.

52 Mary Anderson and colleagues at Collaborative Development Associates (www.cdanic.com) are looking at case studies of communities that prevent violence under conditions that often create violence. Marshall Wallace writes about it in *Global Future*, First Quarter 2005 at (www.globalfuturconline.org).

53 See Herbert Benson and Miriam Klipper, *The Relaxation Response* (New York: HarperTorch, 1976).

54 See "Night Commuters and Soccer in Soroti" in Mennonite Central Committee *Peace Office Newsletter* 34 (April-June 2004).

55 Volkan quoted in "Blind Trust . . . Leader's Actions" p E. See also Volkan, *Blind Trust: Large Groups and Their Leaders.*

56 See *Trauma and Recovery*, p. 176.

57 See *Waking the Tiger*, p 188.

58 See "Emotional First Aid," www.traumahealing.com.

59 See www.emdr.com.

60 See www.thoughtfield.com.

61 See www.traumahealing.com.

62 See http://www.uni-klu.ac.at/~hstockha/neu/html/cabreracruz.htm.

63 See "Forgiveness in Conflict Resolution: Reality and Utility, The Bosnian Experience," (paper presented at the Woodstock Theological Center Colloquium at Georgetown University, October 24, 1997) p. 90.

64 See Botcharova, "Implementation of Track Two Diplomacy" p. 299.

65 See Michael Lapsley sermon, http://www.healingofmemoires.co.za.

66 See "Forgiveness in Conflict Resolution: The Bosnian Experience," p. 82.

67 Ibid.

68 See Botcharova, "Implementation of Track Two Diplomacy" p. 300.

69 Telephone conversation with Bessel A. van der Kolk, February 23, 2005.

70 See Patricia Mathes Cane, *Trauma Healing and Transformation: Awakening a New Heart with Body, Mind, Spirit Practices* (Watsonville, CA: Capacitar, Inc., 2000).

71 See www.peacefultomorrows.org.

72 "Traumawise" is a term coined by Barry Hart, Center for Justice and Peacebuilding, Eastern Mennonite University to mark the wisdom that can emerge from trauma healing and transformation.

73 See "Forgiveness in Conflict Resolution: The Northern Ireland Experience," p.54.

74 See Gutlove and Thompson, *Psychosocial Healing,* for how to structure such meetings.

75 See Bessel A. van der Kolk, "Traumatic Stress Disorder and the Nature of Trauma" in *Healing Trauma: Attachment, Mind, Body, and Brain,* eds. Solomon and Siegel, p.188.

76 See "Forgiveness in Conflict Resolution: The Northern Ireland Experience," p. 69.

77 See Levine, *Waking the Tiger,* p. 194.

78 See Botcharova, "Implementation of Track Two Diplomacy" p. 90-92.

79 See "Forgiveness in Conflict Resolution: The Northern Ireland Experience," pp 5-6.

80 Ibid., p. 28.

81 Ibid. p. 2.

82 Ibid. p.83.

Endnotes

83 Attributed to Berthold Brecht and quoted by Anthony Cary in "Forgiveness in Conflict Resolution: The Northern Ireland Experience," p. 28

84 For more information see Zehr, *Restorative Justice.*

85 Ibid.

86 Adapted from Zehr, *Restorative Justice,* and from an exercise designed by David Dyck who, in turn, drew from Chris Freeman

87 See "Denial, Acknowledgment, and Peacebuilding through Reconciliatory Justice," Te Matahauariki Research Institute at http://lianz.waikato.ac.nz/publications-working.htm.

88 After Wilma's daughter was murdered, she began working as a victim advocate. See Zehr, *Transcending.*

89 See "Forgiveness in Conflict Resolution: The Northern Ireland Experience," p. 82.

90 See Miroslov Volf, "Forgiveness, Reconciliation, and Justice," in *Forgiveness and Reconciliation,* p.39.

91 With thanks to Walter Wink, who asks a series of "What-if" questions related to difficult life events and the use of non-violence. See Chapter 8 in *The Powers That Be.*

92 See Jayne Seminare Docherty and Lisa Schirch of Eastern Mennonite University's Conflict Transformation Center, "A Long-Term Strategy for American Security" available at www.emu.edu/ctp. This paper was written in fall 2001 in answer to the question, "So what would peacebuilders do about 9/11?" It contains short-term, intermediate (10 years), and long-term (50 year) strategies.

93 For nine months, Mohandas Gandhi gave himself to "concerted meditation" to discern the next step in the Indian independence movement in 1930. The vision of the Salt March emerged from this period of prayer and meditation. See Ken Butigan, "Spiritual Practice in the Time of War," in *The Wolf,* the newsletter of *Pace e Bene,* Fall 2004. See www.paceegne.org.

94 See *I'd Rather Teach Peace* (New York: Orbis Books, 2002).

95 See Joseph G. Bock, *Sharpening Conflict Management: Religious Leadership and the Double–Edged Sword* (Westport, CN: Praeger Press, 2001) p. 97.

96 For trainings and resources, see Lisa Schirch, Selected Readings in *Strategic Peacebuilding*.

97 See Peter Ackerman and Jack Duvall, *A Force More Powerful: A Century of Nonviolent Conflict* (New York: St. Martin's Press, 2000) or the videos by the same name, written and produced by Steve York, a production of York and Zimmerman Inc. and WETA Washington D.C.

98 See "Pushing Our Thinking About People Power: How the Differences Among Applications of Nonviolent Action Make Better Strategies Possible," by George Lakey in *ZNet*, April and May 2002. See www.zmag.org.

99 Coleman McCarthy has put together and taught a thought-provoking course on nonviolence, pacifism, and conflict management which he has taught for over 20 years in high schools and universities. See *I'd Rather Teach Peace and All One Peace: Essays on Non-Violence* (New Jersey: Rutgers University Press, 1994).

100 On *News Hour,* British Broadcasting Company, Nov. 3, 2004.

Selected Readings

Fisher, Simon. *Working With Conflict: Skills and Strategies for Action.* (London: Zed Books, 2000).

Gutlove, Paula and Gordon Thompson, eds. *Psychosocial Healing: A Guide for Practitioners.* (Cambridge, MA: Institute for Resource and Security Studies, 2003).

Herman, Judith Lewis. *Trauma and Recovery.* (New York: Basic Books, 1992).

Kleber, Rolf J., Charles R. Figley, and Berthold P.R. Gersons, eds. *Beyond Trauma: Cultural and Societal Dynamics.* (New York: Plenum Press, 1995).

Levine, Peter A. with Ann Frederick. *Waking the Tiger—Healing Trauma: The Innate Capacity to Transform Overwhelming Experiences.* (Berkeley, CA: North Atlantic Books, 1997).

MacNair, Rachel M. *Perpetration-Induced Traumatic Stress: The Psychological Consequences of Killing.* (Westport, CT: Praeger Publishers, 2002).

Schirch, Lisa. *The Little Book of Strategic Peacebuilding.* (Intercourse, PA: Good Books, 2004).

Von Tongeren, Paul. *People Building Peace II: Successful Stories of Civil Society.* (Colorado: Lynne Rienner Publishers, 2005).

Zehr, Howard. *Changing Lenses: A New Focus for Crime and Justice.* Third Edition. (Scottsdale, PA: Herald, 2005).

Zehr, Howard. *The Little Book of Restorative Justice.* (Intercourse, PA: Good Books, 2002).

About the Author

Carolyn Yoder directs the Strategies for Trauma Awareness and Resilience (STAR) a joint program of Eastern Mennonite University's Center for Justice and Peacebuilding (CJP) and Church World Service. She and her family have lived and worked in the Middle East, East and Southern Africa, Asia, the Caribbean, and the U.S. Her experience includes a wide range of trauma work including secondary stress and compassion fatigue in caregivers and survivors of war and torture, both domestically and overseas.

She is a licensed marriage and family counselor, a licensed professional counselor, and a national certified counselor. She holds an M.A. in linguistics from the University of Pittsburgh and an M.A. in counseling psychology from the U.S. International University of San Diego. She and her husband, Rick, are the parents of Katherine, Jessica, and Sara.

A list of Study Questions to enrich group discussion of this book is available (free of charge) on the Good Books website at www.GoodBks.com.

METHOD OF PAYMENT

❏ Check or Money Order
    (*payable to* **Good Books** *in U.S. funds*)

❏ Please charge my:
    ❏ MasterCard   ❏ Visa
    ❏ Discover   ❏ American Express

\# _____

Exp. date _____

Signature _____

Name _____

Address _____

City _____

State _____

Zip _____

Phone _____

Email _____

SHIP TO. (if different)

Name _____

Address _____

City _____

State _____

Zip _____

Mail order to: **Good Books**
P.O. Box 419 • Intercourse, PA 17534-0419
Call toll-free: 800/762-7171
Fax toll-free: 888/768-3433
Prices subject to change.

Group Discounts for

The Little Book of Trauma Healing
ORDER FORM

If you would like to order multiple copies of *The Little Book of Trauma Healing* by Carolyn Yoder for groups you know or are a part of, use this form. (Discounts apply only for more than one copy.)

Photocopy this page as often as you like.

The following discounts apply:

1 copy	$4.95
2-5 copies	$4.45 each (a 10% discount)
6-10 copies	$4.20 each (a 15% discount)
11-20 copies	$3.96 each (a 20% discount)
21-99 copies	$3.45 each (a 30% discount)
100 or more	$2.97 each (a 40% discount)

Free shipping for U.S. orders of 100 or more!

Prices subject to change.

Quantity   *Price*   Total

_____ copies of **Trauma Healing**   @ _____ _____

Shipping & Handling
(U.S. orders only: add 10%; $3.95 minimum) _____
For international orders, please call 800/762-7171, ext. 221

PA residents add 6% sales tax _____

TOTAL _____

800/762-7171 • www.GoodBooks.com